MASTERING GIT FOR VERSION CONTROL

*Optimize Collaborative
Workflows and Conflict
Resolution With Git's
Most Advanced Features*

THOMPSON CARTER

DISCLAIMER

The information contained in this book is provided for educational and informational purposes only and is not intended as professional advice. While every effort has been made to ensure the accuracy of the information herein, the author and publisher make no representations or warranties regarding the completeness, accuracy, or reliability of the content.

The author and publisher disclaim any liability for any direct, indirect, or consequential loss or damage arising from the use of this book or the information it contains, including, but not limited to, errors, omissions, or security vulnerabilities related to code examples, software applications, or any other technical details.

Contents

Chapter 1: Introduction to Version Control

What is Version Control?

Version control, also known as source control or revision control, is a system that helps track and manage changes to files over time. It's a fundamental tool in modern software development, but its applications extend far beyond just code. Writers, designers, scientists, and professionals in various fields can benefit from version control to manage their projects effectively.

At its core, version control serves three primary purposes:

Tracking Changes: It meticulously records who made what changes, when they were made, and why. This historical record is invaluable for understanding the evolution of a project.

Coordinating Work: It enables multiple people to work on the same project simultaneously without interfering with each other's work. This is crucial for team collaboration and productivity.

Reverting and Branching: It allows you to revert to previous versions of your project and create different lines of development. This flexibility is essential for experimenting with new ideas or maintaining multiple versions of a product.

The Essence of Version Control

To truly understand version control, let's break down its key components:

Repository: This is the heart of your version control system. It's a data structure that stores all the versions of your project, along with metadata about each change.

Commit: A commit is a snapshot of your project at a specific point in time. It represents a set of changes that are grouped together logically.

Branch: A branch is an independent line of development. It allows you to work on different features or experiments without affecting the main line of development.

Merge: Merging is the process of integrating changes from one branch into another. It's how separate lines of development are combined.

Clone: A clone is a of a repository. In distributed version control systems like Git, each clone is a full-fledged repository with complete history.

Beyond Software Development

While version control is ubiquitous in software development, its principles can be applied to many other fields:

Writing: Authors can track different drafts of their manuscripts, experiment with alternative plotlines, and collaborate with editors.

Design: Graphic designers can maintain different versions of their artwork, revert to previous designs, and manage assets for different clients.

Scientific Research: Researchers can track changes to their data sets, methodologies, and papers, ensuring reproducibility and collaboration.

Legal Documents: Lawyers can manage different versions of contracts and track changes through negotiations.

Education: Teachers can manage course materials, track syllabus changes over time, and collaborate on curriculum development.

By understanding version control, professionals in these fields and many others can bring more structure, collaboration, and flexibility to their work.

Why Use Version Control?

The benefits of using a version control system are numerous and significant. Let's explore these advantages in detail:

History and Accountability

Complete History: Every change made to your project is recorded, creating a detailed historical record. This history allows you to:

Understand how your project evolved over time

Identify when and why specific changes were introduced

Trace the origin of bugs or issues

Accountability: Each change is associated with a specific author, providing clear accountability. This feature:

Encourages responsibility and ownership of changes

Helps in identifying experts for specific parts of the project

Facilitates code reviews and knowledge sharing

Understanding Context: Commit messages explain why changes were made, providing crucial context for future reference. Good commit messages:

Help future developers (including yourself) understand the rationale behind changes

Serve as documentation for the project's evolution

Aid in quickly identifying the purpose of specific commits when debugging or reviewing changes

Collaboration and Productivity

Concurrent Work: Multiple team members can work on the same project simultaneously without overwriting each other's changes. This concurrent development:

Dramatically increases team productivity

Allows for parallel development of different features

Reduces conflicts and bottlenecks in the development process

Code Review: Version control facilitates systematic code review processes, which:

Improve overall code quality

Promote knowledge sharing within the team

Catch bugs and issues early in the development cycle

Ensure adherence to coding standards and best practices

Branching and Merging: Different lines of development can be pursued in parallel and later merged. This capability:

Allows for experimentation without affecting the main codebase

Facilitates feature-based development workflows

Enables easy management of different versions or editions of a product

Supports hot-fixes and patches for production issues while development continues

Backup and Recovery

Distributed Backups: In distributed version control systems like Git, each developer's local repository serves as a backup of the entire project history. This distribution:

Protects against data loss from server failures

Allows work to continue even when central servers are unavailable

Provides redundancy and resilience to the development process

Easy Recovery: If a mistake is made, you can easily revert to a previous, working state. This ability to recover:

Reduces the fear of making changes or experiments

Allows quick resolution of issues introduced by recent changes

Provides a safety net for development, encouraging innovation

Experimental Freedom: You can experiment with new ideas in separate branches without fear of breaking the main project. This freedom:

Encourages innovation and creativity

Allows for easy comparison between different approaches

Facilitates A/B testing of features or implementations

Project Management

Release Management: Version control helps manage different versions of software releases. This management:

Allows for easy creation and maintenance of different product versions

Facilitates hotfixes and patches for specific releases

Enables clear tracking of what changes are included in each release

Issue Tracking Integration: Many version control systems integrate with issue tracking tools, linking changes to specific tasks or bugs. This integration:

Provides traceability between code changes and project tasks or issues

Facilitates project planning and progress tracking

Helps in generating changelogs and release notes

Continuous Integration/Continuous Deployment (CI/CD): Version control is a fundamental part of modern CI/CD pipelines. This integration:

Automates testing and deployment processes

Ensures that all changes are verified before being merged

Enables rapid and reliable software delivery

Learning and Growth

Code Archaeology: The ability to dig through project history allows developers to understand why certain decisions were made. This archaeological aspect:

Facilitates learning from past decisions and their outcomes

Helps new team members get up to speed quickly

Provides valuable insights for refactoring or redesigning parts of the system

Experimentation and Learning: The safety net provided by version control encourages experimentation. This environment:

Promotes a culture of continuous learning and improvement

Allows developers to try new techniques or technologies without risk

Facilitates mentoring and knowledge sharing within the team

Performance Analysis: By comparing different versions, you can analyze how changes affect the performance of your project. This analysis:

Helps in identifying performance regressions

Facilitates optimization efforts

Provides data for making informed decisions about trade-offs

Brief History of Version Control Systems

The concept of version control has evolved significantly over the years, driven by changing needs in software development and advances in technology. Understanding this evolution provides valuable context for appreciating modern systems like Git.

First Generation: Local VCS

The earliest version control systems were local, meaning they worked on a single computer. These systems were a significant improvement over manual version control (like ing files into numbered folders), but they had limitations in terms of collaboration and distributed work.

Key examples of local VCS include:

SCCS (Source Code Control System):

Developed in 1972 by Marc J. Rochkind at Bell Labs

One of the first VCS, designed for the Unix operating system

Used a centralized model where all versioned files were stored in a special format on disk

Each revision was stored as an initial source file plus a set of deltas (changes)

RCS (Revision Control System):

Created by Walter F. Tichy in 1982 at Purdue University

An improvement over SCCS, with a more efficient storage method

Stored the latest version of a file in full, with reverse deltas for previous versions

Introduced the concept of branching, allowing parallel lines of development

These systems stored patch sets (differences between files) on the local disk, allowing reverting to previous versions. While revolutionary for their time, they had significant limitations:

No support for collaboration between multiple developers

Limited to single file tracking, making it difficult to manage entire projects

No network capability, restricting use to a single computer

Second Generation: Centralized VCS

As networking became more common and software development increasingly became a team effort, centralized version control systems emerged. These systems use a central server to store all versioned files, with clients checking out files from that central place.

Prominent examples include:

CVS (Concurrent Versions System):

Released in 1990 by Dick Grune

Built on top of RCS, adding multi-file, multi-developer capabilities

Introduced the concept of atomic operations, where a single operation could affect multiple files

Allowed developers to work on their own copies and commit changes back to the central repository

Subversion (SVN):

Released in 2000 by CollabNet, Inc.

Designed to be a better CVS, addressing many of its limitations

Introduced the ability to version directories and metadata

Provided better branching and tagging capabilities

Implemented atomic commits, ensuring that a commit either fully succeeds or fully fails

Perforce:

Introduced in 1995

Popular in game development and other industries dealing with large binary files

Known for its performance with large repositories

These centralized systems brought significant advantages:

Enabled collaboration among developers in different locations

Provided a single source of truth for the project

Simplified administration and backup (only one repository to manage)

However, they also had drawbacks:

Single point of failure: If the central server goes down, no one can collaborate or save versioned changes

Limited offline work: Most operations require a connection to the server

Slower for many operations, especially in geographically distributed teams

Third Generation: Distributed VCS

The latest generation of VCS is distributed, where each client has a full of the repository, including its full history. This approach addresses many of the limitations of centralized systems and provides new capabilities.

Key distributed VCS include:

Git:

Created by Linus Torvalds in 2005 for Linux kernel development

Designed for speed, data integrity, and support for distributed, non-linear workflows

Quickly became the most popular VCS due to its flexibility and performance

Mercurial:

Also created in 2005, designed to handle large distributed projects

Known for its simplicity and ease of use

Popular in some large open-source projects and enterprises

Bazaar:

Developed by Canonical, used for Ubuntu development

Designed to be very flexible, supporting both distributed and centralized workflows

Distributed VCS offers several advantages:

Better performance for most operations

Allows offline work, with full version control capabilities

No single point of failure

Encourages experimentation and branching

Supports a wide variety of development workflows

The shift to distributed VCS represents a fundamental change in how we think about version control, emphasizing local operations and flexible collaboration models.

Introduction to Git

While this book will focus primarily on Git, it's worth understanding why Git has become the dominant version control system and how it fits into the broader landscape of version control.

Git's Origins

Git was born out of necessity. In 2005, the relationship between the Linux kernel community and the proprietary VCS they were using, BitKeeper, broke down. This left the community without a VCS that met their specific needs:

Support for distributed development

Ability to handle large projects efficiently

Ensure data integrity

Provide speed for both small and large operations

Linus Torvalds, the creator of Linux, decided to create a new VCS that would meet these requirements. In just a few weeks, Git was born.

Git's Design Philosophy

Git's design was heavily influenced by the needs of the Linux kernel project and Torvalds' experience with other VCS. Key aspects of Git's philosophy include:

Speed: Git operations are designed to be lightning-fast, even for large projects.

Simple Design: The underlying data structures and algorithms are simple, resulting in a system that's powerful yet understandable.

Strong Support for Non-linear Development: Branching and merging are first-class operations in Git.

Distributed: Every Git clone is a full-fledged repository with complete history and version-tracking capabilities.

Ability to Handle Large Projects: Git is designed to handle the Linux kernel project efficiently, which means it can scale to very large projects.

Git's Advantages

Git has several advantages that have contributed to its widespread adoption:

Speed: Git operations are incredibly fast compared to centralized systems. Most operations are local, eliminating network latency.

Distributed Nature: Every clone is a full backup of the repository. This distribution:

Allows for offline work

Provides redundancy and backup

Enables various collaboration workflows

Branching and Merging: Git excels at creating and merging branches. This capability:

Encourages experimentation and feature-based development

Supports complex workflows like GitFlow or GitHub Flow

Makes it easy to maintain multiple versions or configurations

Data Integrity: Git uses SHA-1 hashes to ensure data integrity. Every file and commit is checksummed, making it nearly impossible to change anything in Git without Git knowing about it.

Staging Area: Git's unique staging area (or index) provides fine-grained control over commits. It allows developers to:

Craft precise, logical commits

Review changes before committing

Stage parts of files, enabling partial commits

Open Source: Git is free and open-source, with a large community of contributors. This openness:

Ensures continual improvement and bug fixes

Allows for customization and integration with other tools

Provides a wealth of resources and third-party tools

Git's Adoption

Git has been adopted by many large open-source projects and companies, including:

Linux Kernel

Android

Microsoft (including Windows development)

Facebook

Google

Amazon

Netflix

Its widespread use has made Git proficiency an essential skill for developers and increasingly for professionals in other fields dealing with digital assets.

Git vs Other Version Control Systems

While Git has become the dominant VCS, it's worth understanding how it compares to other systems:

Git vs SVN:

Git is distributed, SVN is centralized

Git has better branching and merging capabilities

Git is generally faster, especially for large projects

SVN can be simpler for those accustomed to centralized workflows

Git vs Mercurial:

Both are distributed VCS with similar capabilities

Git has a larger ecosystem and more widespread adoption

Mercurial is often considered easier to learn

Git offers more flexibility in rewriting history

Git vs Perforce:

Git is distributed, Perforce is centralized (though it offers distributed features)

Perforce traditionally handles large binary files better

Git has better branching and is more flexible

Perforce offers more fine-grained access control

Understanding these differences can help in choosing the right VCS for a project or in migrating between systems.

The Impact of Version Control on Software Development

The adoption of version control, and particularly distributed version control systems like Git, has had a profound impact on how software is developed. Let's explore some of these impacts:

Chapter 2: Getting Started with Git

2.1 Introduction

Now that we understand the importance of version control and have a brief overview of Git's history and advantages, it's time to dive into the practical aspects of using Git. In this chapter, we'll cover everything you need to know to get started with Git, from installation to creating your first repository and making your first commits. By the end of this chapter, you'll have a solid foundation for using Git in your projects and be ready to explore more advanced features.

2.2 Installing Git

Git is available for all major operating systems. The installation process varies depending on your platform, but it's generally straightforward. Let's go through the process for each major operating system.

2.2.1 Installing on Windows

Windows users have several options for installing Git. We'll cover the most common method using the official Git installer.

Download the installer:

Visit the official Git website (https://git-scm.com) and download the latest version for Windows.

You'll usually want the 64-bit version of Git for Windows.

Run the installer:

Double-click the downloaded .exe file to start the installation process.

If prompted by User Account Control, click "Yes" to allow the installer to make changes.

Read and accept the GNU General Public License.

Choose components:

You'll be presented with a list of components to install. The default options are usually sufficient for most users.

Make sure "Git Bash Here" and "Git GUI Here" are selected if you want to use these tools.

If you're unsure about an option, it's generally safe to leave it at the default setting.

Choose the default editor:

Git will occasionally need to open a text editor. Choose your preferred editor from the list.

If you're unsure, Notepad++ or Visual Studio Code are good choices for Windows users.

You can always change this setting later if needed.

Adjusting your PATH environment:

Choose "Git from the command line and also from 3rd-party software" to make Git available from both Git Bash and the Windows Command Prompt.

This option provides the most flexibility for using Git on Windows.

Choosing HTTPS transport backend:

Select "Use the OpenSSL library" for better compatibility with most servers.

Configuring line ending conversions:

Choose "Checkout Windows-style, commit Unix-style line endings" for better compatibility across different operating systems.

This option helps prevent issues when collaborating with developers using different operating systems.

Configuring the terminal emulator:

Choose "Use MinTTY" for a better console experience.

MinTTY provides a more Unix-like terminal experience on Windows.

Configure extra options:

Enable file system caching for better performance.

Enable Git Credential Manager for easier authentication with remote repositories.

Install:

Click "Install" to start the installation process.

Wait for the installation to complete.

After installation, you can open Git Bash or the regular Command Prompt to start using Git.

2.2.2 Installing on macOS

macOS users have several options for installing Git. We'll cover three common methods.

Using Homebrew (recommended):

Homebrew is a popular package manager for macOS.

If you don't have Homebrew installed, install it first by following the instructions at https://brew.sh/

Open Terminal and run: `brew install git`

This method makes it easy to keep Git updated in the future.

Using the installer:

Visit https://git-scm.com and download the latest version for macOS.

Double-click the downloaded .dmg file.

Follow the installation instructions in the opened window.

This method provides a straightforward graphical installation process.

Using Xcode Command Line Tools:

If you have Xcode installed or plan to do iOS or macOS development, this method is convenient.

Open Terminal and run: `xcode-select --install`

Follow the prompts to install the Xcode Command Line Tools, which includes Git.

This method ensures Git is installed alongside other developer tools you might need.

After installation, you can open Terminal to start using Git.

2.2.3 Installing on Linux

The process for installing Git on Linux varies depending on your distribution, but it's typically done through your distribution's package manager. Here are instructions for some popular distributions:

For Debian/Ubuntu:

Open Terminal and run:

```
sudo apt update
sudo apt install git
```

Enter your password when prompted.

For Fedora:

Open Terminal and run: `sudo dnf install git`

Enter your password when prompted.

For CentOS/RHEL:

Open Terminal and run: `sudo yum install git`

Enter your password when prompted.

For Arch Linux:

Open Terminal and run: `sudo pacman -S git`

Enter your password when prompted.

After installation, you can use Git directly from the Terminal.

2.2.4 Verifying the Installation

Regardless of your operating system, after installation, you should verify that Git is correctly installed:

Open a terminal or command prompt.

Run the following command:

```
git --version
```

You should see output similar to:

```
git version 2.30.1
```

(The exact version number may be different.)

If you see this output, congratulations! Git is successfully installed on your system.

2.3 Basic Git Configuration

Before you start using Git, you should configure some basic settings. Git uses a series of configuration files, but for now, we'll focus on the global configuration.

2.3.1 Setting Your Identity

The first thing you should do is set your user name and email address. This is important because Git embeds this information into every commit you make. To set these:

```
git config --global user.name "Your Name"

git        config        --global        user.email
"your.email@example.com"
```

Replace "Your Name" and "your.email@example.com" with your actual name and email.

2.3.2 Choosing Your Default Editor

Git sometimes needs to open a text editor, for example, to edit commit messages. You can configure which editor it uses:

```
git config --global core.editor "code --wait"
```

This example sets Visual Studio Code as the default editor. Replace "code" with the command for your preferred editor. Some common alternatives:

For Notepad++ on Windows: `"'C:/Program Files/Notepad++/notepad++.exe' -multiInst -notabbar -nosession -noPlugin"`

For Sublime Text: `"subl -w"`

For Atom: `"atom --wait"`

For vim: `"vim"`

For nano: `"nano -w"`

2.3.3 Configuring Line Endings

Different operating systems handle line endings differently. To avoid issues when collaborating across different OSes, you can configure Git to handle line endings automatically:

On Windows:

```
git config --global core.autocrlf true
```

On macOS and Linux:

```
git config --global core.autocrlf input
```

2.3.4 Configuring Color Output

Git can color its output to make it easier to read. To enable this:

```
git config --global color.ui auto
```

2.3.5 Checking Your Settings

To check your configuration settings, use:

```
git config --list
```

This will display all your current Git settings.

2.3.6 Getting Help

If you ever need help with a Git command, you can access the manual page for that command by running:

```
git help <command>
```

For example, `git help config` will give you detailed information about the `git config` command.

2.4 Understanding Git Basics

Before we create our first repository, let's understand some fundamental Git concepts.

2.4.1 The Three States

Git has three main states that your files can reside in:

Modified: You have changed the file, but have not committed it to your database yet.

Staged: You have marked a modified file in its current version to go into your next commit snapshot.

Committed: The data is safely stored in your local database.

Understanding these states is crucial for effective use of Git.

2.4.2 The Three Main Sections of a Git Project

This leads us to the three main sections of a Git project:

Working Directory: This is where you modify your files. It's a single checkout of one version of the project.

Staging Area: This is a file, generally contained in your Git directory, that stores information about what will go into your next commit. It's sometimes referred to as the "index".

Git Directory: This is where Git stores the metadata and object database for your project. This is what gets copied when you clone a repository from another computer.

2.4.3 The Basic Git Workflow

The basic Git workflow goes something like this:

You modify files in your working directory.

You stage the files, adding snapshots of them to your staging area.

You do a commit, which takes the files as they are in the staging area and stores that snapshot permanently to your Git directory.

2.5 Creating Your First Git Repository

Now that we understand the basics, let's create our first Git repository.

2.5.1 Initializing a Repository in an Existing Directory

If you have a project directory that you want to start tracking with Git:

Open a terminal or command prompt.

Navigate to your project's directory:

```
cd path/to/your/project
```

Initialize the repository:

```
git init
```

This creates a new subdirectory named .git that contains all of your necessary repository files — a Git repository skeleton. At this point, nothing in your project is tracked yet.

2.5.2 Creating a New Repository from Scratch

If you're starting a new project:

Create a new directory for your project:

```
mkdir my_new_project

cd my_new_project
```

Initialize the repository:

```
git init
```

2.5.3 Understanding the .git Directory

The `.git` directory is where Git stores all the information about your repository. Let's look at its contents:

```
ls -la .git
```

You'll see several files and directories:

`config`: File containing your project-specific configuration options.

`description`: File used by GitWeb program (you can ignore this).

`HEAD`: File that points to the branch you currently have checked out.

`hooks/`: Directory containing client- or server-side hook scripts.

`info/`: Directory containing global excludes.

`objects/`: Directory that stores all the content for your database.

`refs/`: Directory that stores pointers to commit objects in that data (branches, tags, remotes, and more).

Don't worry if this seems complex now. As you use Git, you'll become more familiar with these components.

2.6 Making Your First Commit

Now that we have a repository, let's make our first commit.

2.6.1 Creating a New File

Let's create a simple text file:

```
echo "Hello, Git!" > hello.txt
```

2.6.2 Checking the Status

To see which files are in which state, run:

```
git status
```

You should see something like:

```
On branch master


No commits yet


Untracked files:

(use "git add <file>..." to include in what will be
committed)

hello.txt



nothing added to commit but untracked files present
(use "git add" to track)
```

This tells us that `hello.txt` is untracked, meaning Git sees a file that didn't exist in the previous snapshot.

2.6.3 Staging the File

To start tracking the new file, use the `git add` command:

```
git add hello.txt
```

If you run `git status` again, you'll see that the file is now staged:

```
On branch master
```

39

```
No commits yet


Changes to be committed:

(use "git rm --cached <file>..." to unstage)

new file:   hello.txt
```

2.6.4 Committing the File

Now that your file is staged, you can commit it:

```
git commit -m "Initial commit: Add hello.txt"
```

The -m flag allows you to provide a commit message directly on the command line.

After running this command, you should see something like:

```
[master (root-commit) 5ec1e43] Initial commit: Add
hello.txt

1 file changed, 1 insertion(+)

create mode 100644 hello.txt
```

Congratulations! You've just made your first Git commit.

2.7 Viewing the Commit History

To see the history of commits, use the `git log` command:

```
git log
```

You should see something like:

```
commit      5ec1e43b0f7ec6f3123456789abcdef0123456789
(HEAD -> master)

Author: Your Name <your.email@example.com>

Date:    Mon Jan 1 12:00:00 2024 +0000


Initial commit: Add hello.txt
```

This shows:

The full SHA-1 hash of the commit

The author of the commit

The date of the commit

The commit message

As you make more commits, they will appear in this log, with the most recent commits at the top.

2.8 Making Changes and Committing Them

Let's make a change to our file and commit it.

2.8.1 Modifying the File

Open `hello.txt` in your text editor and change its contents:

```
echo "Hello, Git! I'm learning version control." >
hello.txt
```

2.8.2 Checking the Status

Run `git status` again:

```
On branch master

Changes not staged for commit:

(use "git add <file>..." to update what will be
committed)

(use "git restore <file>..." to discard changes in
working directory)

modified:   hello.txt


no changes added to commit (use "git add" and/or "git
commit -a")
```

This tells us that `hello.txt` has been modified but not yet staged.

2.8.3 Viewing the Differences

To see what you've changed but not yet staged, run:

```
git diff
```

This will show you the exact lines that were added and removed.

2.8.4 Staging and Committing the Changes

Stage the changes:

```
git add hello.txt
```

And commit them:

```
git commit -m "Update hello.txt with more content"
```

2.9 Understanding the Git Workflow

Let's recap the basic Git workflow:

Modify files in your working directory.

Stage the files, adding snapshots of them to your staging area.

Commit your changes, which takes the files as they are in the staging area and stores that snapshot permanently to your Git directory.

This workflow allows you to group related changes into cohesive commits, giving you fine-grained control over the history of your project.

2.10 Best Practices for Commits

As you start using Git, keep these best practices in mind:

Commit often: Make small, frequent commits rather than large, infrequent ones. This makes it easier to track changes and revert if necessary.

Write meaningful commit messages: Your future self (and others) will thank you. A good format is:

```
Short (50 chars or less) summary of changes


More detailed explanatory text, if necessary. Wrap it
to about 72

characters or so. The blank line separating the
summary from the body
```

is critical (unless you omit the body entirely).

Further paragraphs come after blank lines.

Bullet points are okay, too

Typically a hyphen or asterisk is used for the bullet

Chapter 3: Branching and Merging in Git

3.1 Introduction to Branching

Branching is one of Git's most powerful features. It allows you to diverge from the main line of development and continue to do work without messing with that main line. In essence, a branch in Git is simply a lightweight movable pointer to a commit. This makes branching in Git incredibly fast and easy to use.

3.1.1 Why Use Branches?

Branches serve several important purposes in Git:

Parallel Development: You can work on different features or experiments simultaneously without affecting the main codebase.

Isolation: Bugs and experimental code are contained within a branch, keeping the main codebase stable.

Collaboration: Different team members can work on different features in separate branches.

Organization: Branches can represent different stages of development (e.g., development, staging, production).

3.1.2 The Default Branch: Master/Main

When you initialize a Git repository, it creates a default branch. Traditionally, this branch was called "master", but many projects now use "main" as the default branch name for inclusivity reasons. You can change the default branch name in your Git configuration:

```
git config --global init.defaultBranch main
```

For consistency, we'll use "main" throughout this chapter, but be aware that you might encounter "master" in older repositories or documentation.

3.2 Creating and Switching Branches

Let's dive into how to create and switch between branches.

3.2.1 Creating a New Branch

To create a new branch, use the `git branch` command:

```
git branch feature-branch
```

This creates a new branch called `feature-branch`, but doesn't switch to it.

3.2.2 Switching to a Branch

To switch to a branch, use the `git checkout` command:

```
git checkout feature-branch
```

3.2.3 Creating and Switching in One Command

You can create a new branch and switch to it in one command using:

```
git checkout -b new-feature-branch
```

This creates `new-feature-branch` and switches to it immediately.

3.2.4 Listing Branches

To see a list of all branches in your repository:

```
git branch
```

The current branch will be marked with an asterisk (*).

3.2.5 Deleting a Branch

To delete a branch:

```
git branch -d branch-to-delete
```

Note that you can't delete the branch you're currently on, and Git won't let you delete a branch that has unmerged changes by default.

3.3 Working with Branches

Once you've created a branch, you can work on it just like you would on the main branch. Let's walk through a typical workflow.

3.3.1 Making Changes in a Branch

Switch to your feature branch:

```
git checkout feature-branch
```

Make some changes to your files.

Stage and commit your changes:

```
git add .
git commit -m "Implement new feature"
```

3.3.2 Switching Between Branches

You can switch between branches at any time:

```
git checkout main
```

```
git checkout feature-branch
```

Git will update your working directory to match the branch you're switching to.

3.3.3 Comparing Branches

To see the differences between two branches:

```
git diff main feature-branch
```

This shows the differences between the tips of the `main` and `feature-branch` branches.

3.4 Merging Branches

Once you've completed work in a branch, you'll want to incorporate those changes back into the main branch. This process is called merging.

3.4.1 Fast-Forward Merge

If the branch you're merging in is directly ahead of the branch you're on, Git will simply move the pointer forward. This is called a "fast-forward" merge.

Switch to the branch you want to merge into:

```
git checkout main
```

Merge the feature branch:

```
git merge feature-branch
```

3.4.2 Three-Way Merge

If the branch you're merging has diverged from the branch you're on, Git will perform a "three-way merge", using the two snapshots pointed to by the branch tips and their common ancestor.

Switch to the branch you want to merge into:

```
git checkout main
```

Merge the feature branch:

```
git merge feature-branch
```

Git will create a new "merge commit" if there are no conflicts.

3.4.3 Resolving Merge Conflicts

Sometimes, Git can't automatically merge changes. This happens when the same part of the same file has been modified differently in the two branches you're merging. When this occurs:

Git will pause the merge process and mark the conflicting areas in the relevant files.

52

Open the conflicting file(s) and look for the conflict markers:

```
<<<<<<< HEAD
Your changes
=======
Changes from the branch you're merging
>>>>>>> feature-branch
```

Edit the file to resolve the conflict, removing the conflict markers.

Stage the resolved file:

```
git add resolved-file.txt
```

Complete the merge by creating a merge commit:

```
git commit -m "Merge feature-branch, resolving conflicts"
```

3.5 Rebasing

Rebasing is an alternative to merging. Instead of creating a new commit that combines two branches, rebasing moves or combines a sequence of commits to a new base commit.

3.5.1 Basic Rebasing

Switch to the branch you want to rebase:

```
git checkout feature-branch
```

Rebase onto the main branch:

```
git rebase main
```

This moves the entire `feature-branch` to begin on the tip of the `main` branch.

3.5.2 When to Rebase vs. Merge

Use rebase for cleaning up your local commit history before sharing your work.

Use merge for integrating completed features, especially in shared branches.

3.5.3 The Golden Rule of Rebasing

Never rebase commits that have been pushed to a public repository. Rebasing changes history, which can cause problems for other collaborators.

3.6 Advanced Branch Management

As you become more comfortable with branching, you can use more advanced techniques to manage your workflow.

3.6.1 Cherry-Picking

Cherry-picking allows you to pick individual commits from one branch and apply them to another.

```
git cherry-pick <commit-hash>
```

This is useful when you want to apply a specific change without merging the entire branch.

3.6.2 Using Tags

Tags are references that point to specific points in Git history. Unlike branches, tags don't change once they're created. They're useful for marking release points.

To create a tag:

```
git tag v1.0.0
```

To create an annotated tag with a message:

```
git tag -a v1.0.0 -m "Release version 1.0.0"
```

3.6.3 Branch Naming Conventions

Adopting a consistent branch naming convention can help keep your repository organized:

`feature/`: for new features (e.g., `feature/user-authentication`)

`bugfix/`: for bug fixes (e.g., `bugfix/login-error`)

`hotfix/`: for quick fixes to production (e.g., `hotfix/security-patch`)

`release/`: for release branches (e.g., `release/v1.1.0`)

3.6.4 Git Flow

Git Flow is a popular branching model that defines a strict branching structure designed around project releases. It involves these main branches:

`main`: stores the official release history

`develop`: serves as an integration branch for features

`feature/`: for developing new features

`release/`: for preparing releases

`hotfix/`: for quickly patching production releases

While powerful, Git Flow can be complex for smaller projects or teams practicing continuous delivery.

3.7 Best Practices for Branching and Merging

As you work with branches, keep these best practices in mind:

Branch Often: Create branches for each new feature, bug fix, or experiment.

Keep Branches Short-Lived: Merge or delete branches once their purpose has been fulfilled.

Use Descriptive Branch Names: Choose names that describe the work being done in the branch.

Regularly Merge or Rebase from the Main Branch: Keep your feature branches up-to-date to minimize merge conflicts.

Review Before Merging: Use pull requests or code reviews before merging branches into main.

Delete Stale Branches: Remove branches that are no longer needed to keep your repository clean.

Don't Rewrite Public History: Avoid rebasing or force-pushing to branches that others are working on.

Test Before and After Merging: Ensure your changes work in isolation and after integration.

3.8 Visualizing Branches

Understanding the state of your branches can be challenging, especially in complex projects. Git provides several tools to help visualize your branch structure.

3.8.1 Using git log

The `git log` command can show you a text-based representation of your branch history:

```
git log --oneline --decorate --graph --all
```

This command shows:

`--oneline`: Condenses each commit to a single line

`--decorate`: Shows which branch each commit is on

`--graph`: Draws a text-based graph of commits

`--all`: Shows all branches, not just the current one

3.8.2 GUI Tools

Many GUI tools provide visual representations of your Git history, including:

GitKraken

Sourcetree

GitHub Desktop

Visual Studio Code's Git Graph extension

These tools can make it easier to understand complex branching structures and merge histories.

3.9 Common Branching Strategies

Different teams and projects may adopt different branching strategies based on their needs. Here are a few common strategies:

3.9.1 GitHub Flow

A simple, lightweight workflow:

Create a branch from `main` for each new feature or bug fix

Commit changes to the branch

Open a pull request

Discuss and review the code

Deploy and test

Merge to `main` and delete the branch

3.9.2 GitLab Flow

Similar to GitHub Flow, but with environment branches:

`main` for development

`pre-production` for staging

`production` for released code

3.9.3 Trunk-Based Development

A source-control branching model where developers collaborate on code in a single branch (the "trunk"), resisting any pressure to create other long-lived development branches.

3.10 Conclusion

Branching and merging are fundamental to Git and key to unlocking its full potential. They allow for parallel development, experimentation, and collaboration. By understanding these concepts and practicing the techniques we've covered, you'll be well on your way to mastering Git.

Remember, the power of branching lies in its flexibility. As you become more comfortable with these concepts, you'll develop workflows that suit your project's specific needs. Don't be afraid to experiment with different branching strategies to find what works best for you and your team.

In the next chapter, we'll explore how to collaborate with others using remote repositories, building on the branching and merging concepts we've covered here.

Chapter 5: Advanced Git Techniques

Introduction

As you become more proficient with Git, you'll discover that it offers a wealth of advanced features and techniques that can significantly enhance your workflow. This chapter delves into these advanced concepts, providing you with the knowledge to leverage Git's full potential. We'll explore powerful commands, discuss complex scenarios, and introduce you to techniques that can help you manage large projects more effectively. By mastering these advanced techniques, you'll be able to handle even the most challenging version control situations with confidence.

Rewriting History

One of Git's most powerful (and potentially dangerous) features is its ability to rewrite history. This can be incredibly useful for cleaning up your commit history before sharing your work, but it should be used with caution, especially on public branches.

Interactive Rebasing

Interactive rebasing is a powerful tool that allows you to modify commits in many ways. You can reorder, edit, squash, or even delete commits entirely.

To start an interactive rebase, use the following command:

```
git rebase -i <commit>
```

Replace `<commit>` with the commit hash or reference (like HEAD~3) that you want to start rebasing from.

This will open your default text editor with a list of commits and commands. You can change the command (pick, reword, edit, squash, fixup, drop) for each commit to modify how it's treated during the rebase.

For example, to squash several commits into one:

```
pick f7f3f6d Change button color

squash 310154e Update button padding

squash a5f4a0d Refactor button component
```

This would combine the second and third commits into the first one.

Remember, interactive rebasing rewrites history, so only use it on commits that haven't been pushed to a shared repository.

Commit Amending

Sometimes, you might want to modify your most recent commit. Maybe you forgot to add a file, or you want to change the commit message. The --amend flag allows you to do this:

```
git commit --amend
```

This opens your editor to modify the most recent commit message. If you've staged changes, they'll be added to the amended commit.

To add forgotten files without changing the commit message:

```
git add forgotten_file
git commit --amend --no-edit
```

Again, only amend commits that haven't been pushed to a shared repository.

Cherry-Picking

Cherry-picking allows you to apply the changes introduced by some existing commits. This can be useful when you want to pick specific changes from one branch and apply them to another.

To cherry-pick a commit:

```
git cherry-pick <commit-hash>
```

This creates a new commit on your current branch with the changes from the specified commit.

You can cherry-pick multiple commits:

```
git cherry-pick <commit-hash-1> <commit-hash-2>
```

If you just want to apply the changes without creating a new commit, use the `--no-commit` or `-n` flag:

```
git cherry-pick -n <commit-hash>
```

Resetting

The `git reset` command is a powerful tool for undoing changes. It moves the current branch tip backward to a specified commit, essentially rewriting the commit history.

There are three main options for reset:

Soft reset (`--soft`): Moves the HEAD to the specified commit, but leaves the changes in the staging area.

Mixed reset (default): Moves the HEAD and updates the staging area with the contents of the specified commit.

Hard reset (`--hard`): Moves the HEAD, updates the staging area, and updates the working directory to match the specified commit.

For example, to undo the last commit but keep the changes staged:

```
git reset --soft HEAD~1
```

To completely undo the last commit and all changes:

```
git reset --hard HEAD~1
```

Be very careful with `git reset`, especially `--hard`, as it can result in losing work if used incorrectly.

Advanced Branching Techniques

While we covered basic branching in earlier chapters, there are some advanced branching techniques that can be very useful in complex projects.

Orphan Branches

An orphan branch is a branch that starts with no commit history. This can be useful for things like creating a new `gh-pages` branch for GitHub Pages.

To create an orphan branch:

```
git checkout --orphan new-branch
```

This creates a new branch with no parents. The working directory remains unchanged, but none of the files are staged for commit.

Worktrees

Git worktrees allow you to check out multiple branches of the same repository into different directories. This can be useful when you need to work on multiple branches simultaneously.

To add a new worktree:

```
git worktree add ../path-to-new-directory branch-name
```

This checks out the specified branch into a new directory. You can now work on this branch independently of your main working directory.

To list worktrees:

```
git worktree list
```

To remove a worktree:

```
git worktree remove path-to-worktree
```

Reflog

The reflog is a mechanism Git uses to record updates applied to branch tips and other references. It's like a safety net, allowing you to recover lost commits or branches.

To view the reflog:

```
git reflog
```

This shows a log of all reference updates in the repository. You can use this to find lost commits or branches and recover them.

For example, to recover a branch that was accidentally deleted:

```
git checkout -b recovered-branch <sha>
```

Where <sha> is the commit hash of the branch tip before it was deleted, found in the reflog.

Submodules and Subtrees

When working on large projects, you might need to include other projects within your project. Git provides two main ways to do this: submodules and subtrees.

Submodules

Submodules allow you to keep a Git repository as a subdirectory of another Git repository. This lets you clone another repository into your project and keep your commits separate.

To add a submodule:

```
git submodule add https://github.com/example/repo.git
path/to/submodule
```

This creates a new directory at the specified path, clones the repository there, and adds it as a submodule.

When cloning a project with submodules, you need to initialize and update them:

```
git submodule init

git submodule update
```

Or, you can clone with submodules in one command:

```
git                clone              --recurse-submodules
https://github.com/example/repo.git
```

Submodules can be tricky to work with, as they point to a specific commit in the submodule's repository. When you want to update a submodule to a newer version:

```
cd path/to/submodule
```

```
git fetch

git checkout master

git pull

cd ../..

git add path/to/submodule

git commit -m "Update submodule to latest"
```

Subtrees

Subtrees are an alternative to submodules. They allow you to insert another project into a subdirectory of your main project.

To add a subtree:

```
git      subtree      add      --prefix=path/to/subtree
https://github.com/example/repo.git master --squash
```

This adds the `master` branch of the specified repository as a subtree in the specified path.

To update a subtree:

```
git      subtree      pull      --prefix=path/to/subtree
https://github.com/example/repo.git master --squash
```

Subtrees are generally easier to use than submodules, as they don't require special commands to clone or update.

However, they can make your repository larger, as the entire history of the subtree is included in your main repository.

Git Hooks

Git hooks are scripts that Git executes before or after events such as: commit, push, and receive. They can be used to enforce certain workflows, automatically run tests, or perform custom actions at specific points in your Git workflow.

Hook scripts are stored in the `.git/hooks` directory of your Git repository. To enable a hook, rename the sample file (removing the .sample extension) and make it executable.

Some common hooks include:

`pre-commit`: Runs before a commit is created. Can be used to run tests or lint code.

`prepare-commit-msg`: Runs after the default commit message is created but before the commit message editor is started.

`post-commit`: Runs after a commit is created. Can be used for notifications.

`pre-push`: Runs before a push is started. Can be used to run tests or prevent pushing to certain branches.

Here's an example of a simple `pre-commit` hook that runs tests before allowing a commit:

bash

```sh
#!/bin/sh



npm test

# $? stores exit value of the last command

if [ $? -ne 0 ]; then

echo "Tests must pass before commit!"

exit 1

fi
```

Remember, hooks are not transferred with `git clone` of a project. You'll need to distribute them manually or include them in your project files (outside of `.git`) with instructions for installation.

Advanced Merging Techniques

While we covered basic merging in earlier chapters, there are some advanced merging techniques that can be useful in complex situations.

Merge Strategies

Git has several merge strategies available. The default is usually the "recursive" strategy, but you can specify others:

`ours`: Forces conflicting hunks to be auto-resolved cleanly by favoring the current branch version.

`theirs`: The opposite of `ours`, favors the version being merged in.

`octopus`: Can merge multiple branches at once.

To use a specific merge strategy:

```
git merge -s <strategy> <branch>
```

Merge Options

You can also pass options to the merge command to change its behavior:

`--no-ff`: Always create a merge commit, even if a fast-forward is possible.

`--squash`: Squash all commits from the merging branch into a single commit.

`-X ignore-space-change`: Ignore whitespace changes when resolving conflicts.

For example:

Resolving Complex Merge Conflicts

Sometimes, you'll encounter complex merge conflicts that aren't easily resolved. Here are some techniques to handle these:

Use `git mergetool`: This opens a visual diff tool to help resolve conflicts.

Use `git checkout --ours` or `git checkout --theirs` to choose one version over another for a specific file.

Use `git log --merge` to see commits that touched a file with merge conflicts.

Remember, communication with your team is crucial when resolving complex merge conflicts to ensure everyone's work is properly integrated.

Chapter 6: Git Workflows and Project Management

Introduction

In the previous chapters, we've explored the technical aspects of Git, from basic commands to advanced techniques. Now, we'll shift our focus to how Git is used in real-world scenarios, particularly in the context of project management and team collaboration. This chapter will delve into various Git workflows, discuss how to integrate Git with project management methodologies, and explore best practices for using Git in large-scale projects.

Understanding Git Workflows

A Git workflow is a recipe or recommendation for how to use Git to accomplish work in a consistent and productive manner. Git workflows encourage developers and DevOps teams to leverage Git effectively and consistently. Git offers a lot of flexibility in how users manage changes, and several workflows have emerged as best practices depending on the size of the team, the project, and the deployment model.

The Centralized Workflow

The Centralized Workflow is the simplest of all workflows and is often the starting point for teams transitioning from SVN. In this model:

There is a single "central" repository.

Developers clone the central repository, make changes locally, and push their new commits directly back to the central repository.

There is only one main branch, often called "master" or "main".

This workflow works well for small teams or projects with few conflicts. However, it can lead to problems when multiple developers try to push changes to the same branch simultaneously.

Pros:

Simple to understand and implement

Works well for small teams or projects

Cons:

Can lead to conflicts in busy repositories

Lacks isolation for new features or experiments

Feature Branch Workflow

The Feature Branch Workflow builds on the Centralized Workflow by requiring developers to create a new branch for each feature or fix. This approach:

Keeps the main branch clean and always deployable

Makes it easier to conduct code reviews via pull requests

Allows for experimentation without affecting the main codebase

In this workflow:

Developers create a new branch for each feature or bug fix

Work is done on these feature branches

When complete, the developer opens a pull request

After code review and any necessary changes, the feature branch is merged into the main branch

This workflow is popular because it strikes a balance between simplicity and isolation of work.

Pros:

Keeps the main branch clean

Facilitates code reviews

Allows for experimentation

Cons:

Can lead to long-lived branches if not managed properly

May require more Git knowledge from team members

Gitflow Workflow

The Gitflow Workflow is a robust framework for managing larger projects. Gitflow defines a strict branching model designed around the project release. It assigns very specific roles to different branches and defines how and when they should interact.

In Gitflow:

The 'master' branch stores the official release history

A parallel 'develop' branch serves as an integration branch for features

Feature branches are used for new features and bug fixes

Release branches prepare new production releases

Hotfix branches allow for emergency fixes to production releases

While powerful, Gitflow can be complex and may be overkill for smaller projects or teams practicing continuous delivery.

Pros:

Provides a robust framework for managing releases

Well-suited for projects with a scheduled release cycle

Allows for parallel development of multiple features

Cons:

Can be complex to understand and implement

May introduce unnecessary overhead for smaller projects

Can lead to merge conflicts in long-lived branches

Forking Workflow

The Forking Workflow is fundamentally different from the other workflows. Instead of using a single server-side repository to act as the "central" codebase, it gives every developer their own server-side repository. This means that each contributor has not one, but two Git repositories: a private local one and a public server-side one.

The main steps in a Forking Workflow are:

A developer 'forks' an 'official' server-side repository, creating their own server-side

The new server-side is cloned to their local system

A Git remote path for the 'official' repository is added to the local clone

A new local feature branch is created

The developer makes changes on the new branch

New commits are pushed to their own public repository

The developer opens a pull request from the new branch to the 'official' repository

The pull request gets approved and merged by the project maintainer

This workflow is often seen in open source projects, as it allows contributions from developers who may not have push access to the main repository.

Pros:

Allows for contributions from a wide range of developers

Provides a clear separation between the official codebase and contributor's work

Reduces the need for complex permission management on the main repository

Cons:

Can be complex to set up and manage

May lead to divergence if the main repository changes rapidly

Requires more Git operations for simple changes

Trunk-Based Development

Trunk-Based Development is a source-control branching model where developers collaborate on code in a single branch called 'trunk', resist any pressure to create other long-lived development branches, and therefore avoid merge hell, do not break the build, and live happily ever after.

Key aspects of Trunk-Based Development include:

Short-lived feature branches, if used at all

Developers integrate their work to the trunk at least once a day

High reliance on feature toggles and other techniques to keep the trunk always releasable

Emphasis on automated testing and continuous integration

This approach is gaining popularity, especially in teams practicing continuous delivery or continuous deployment.

Pros:

Simplifies the development process

Reduces merge conflicts and integration problems

Facilitates continuous integration and delivery

Cons:

Requires a high level of discipline from the development team

May be challenging for less experienced Git users

Can be difficult to implement in larger teams or more complex projects

Choosing the Right Workflow

Selecting the right Git workflow depends on several factors:

Team size and structure

Project complexity

Release schedule

Deployment model (e.g., continuous delivery vs. scheduled releases)

Team's Git expertise

It's important to remember that these workflows are not mutually exclusive, and many teams use hybrid approaches that combine elements from different workflows. The key is to find a workflow that enhances your team's productivity and suits your project's needs.

Integrating Git with Project Management

Git isn't just a version control system; when used effectively, it can be a powerful tool for project management. Here are some ways to integrate Git into your project management practices:

Issue Tracking

Many Git hosting platforms (like GitHub, GitLab, and Bitbucket) provide built-in issue tracking. You can link issues to specific commits, branches, or pull requests. This creates a clear connection between the problem, the solution, and the code changes.

Best practices for issue tracking with Git:

Use a consistent naming convention for branches that includes the issue number (e.g., `feature/123-add-login-page`)

Reference issue numbers in commit messages (e.g., "Fix login bug #456")

Use keywords in pull request descriptions to automatically close issues when merged (e.g., "Closes #789")

Project Boards

Project boards (like GitHub Projects or GitLab Boards) allow you to create Kanban-style boards directly linked to your Git repository. You can move issues and pull requests through columns representing different stages of your workflow.

Tips for using project boards:

Create columns that match your development process (e.g., To Do, In Progress, Review, Done)

Use automation to move cards based on Git events (e.g., move to 'Review' when a pull request is opened)

Use labels to categorize and filter issues and pull requests

Milestones

Milestones allow you to group issues and pull requests into broader goals or releases. You can set due dates for milestones and track progress towards completion.

Effective use of milestones:

Create a milestone for each planned release or sprint

Assign relevant issues and pull requests to the milestone

Use the milestone's progress bar to track completion

Code Reviews

Pull requests facilitate code reviews, an essential part of many development workflows. Good code review practices can improve code quality, share knowledge, and catch bugs early.

Code review best practices:

Keep pull requests small and focused

Use pull request templates to ensure all necessary information is provided

Automate checks (e.g., linting, tests) to run on pull requests

Encourage constructive and respectful feedback

Continuous Integration/Continuous Deployment (CI/CD)

Git can be tightly integrated with CI/CD pipelines. Many CI/CD tools can be triggered by Git events (like pushes or pull requests) and can update the status of commits or pull requests based on build and test results.

CI/CD integration tips:

Set up automated tests to run on every push

Use branch protection rules to require passing CI checks before merging

Automate deployments based on Git events (e.g., deploy to staging when merged to develop, deploy to production when tagged)

Documentation

Git repositories aren't just for code. They're also excellent places to store and version control documentation. Many teams use markdown files in their Git repositories for documentation, which can be automatically rendered on platforms like GitHub or GitLab.

Documentation best practices:

Keep a README.md file in the root of your repository with essential project information

Use a docs/ directory for more detailed documentation

Consider using GitHub Pages or similar tools to publish documentation directly from your repository

Git for Large-Scale Projects

As projects grow in size and complexity, effectively using Git becomes more challenging. Here are some strategies for managing Git in large-scale projects:

Monorepo vs. Multirepo

One of the first decisions for large projects is whether to use a monorepo (one large repository for all code) or a multirepo (multiple smaller repositories) approach.

Monorepo pros:

Easier to manage dependencies and share code

Simplified CI/CD setup

Easier to refactor across project boundaries

Monorepo cons:

Can become very large, leading to slow clones and operations

May require specialized tools to manage

Can be overwhelming for new team members

Multirepo pros:

Clearer ownership and access control

Faster Git operations on individual repositories

Easier to understand for new team members

Multirepo cons:

More complex dependency management

More challenging to make cross-cutting changes

May lead to code duplication

Managing Large Repositories

If you're working with a large repository:

Use shallow clones (`git clone --depth 1`) for faster initial clones

Use Git LFS (Large File Storage) for large binary files

Regularly clean up old branches and use `git gc` to optimize the repository

Branch Management

In large projects, branch management becomes crucial:

Use a clear naming convention for branches (e.g., `feature/`, `bugfix/`, `hotfix/`)

Regularly delete merged branches

Consider using tools like GitLab's "merge when pipeline succeeds" feature to manage busy branches

Code Organization

Organize your code in a way that makes sense for your project:

Use clear, consistent directory structures

Consider using Git submodules or subtrees for shared components

Use .gitignore files effectively to exclude unnecessary files

Team Structure

For large teams:

Use CODEOWNERS files to automatically request reviews from the right people

Consider using GitHub's "required reviewers" feature

Use teams and roles in your Git hosting platform to manage permissions

Git Best Practices for Project Management

To wrap up, here are some overall best practices for using Git in project management:

Commit often: Make small, frequent commits rather than large, infrequent ones

Write clear commit messages: Use a consistent format and provide context

Use branches effectively: Create a new branch for each feature or bug fix

Keep the main branch stable: Only merge thoroughly tested code into the main branch

Automate where possible: Use CI/CD, automated tests, and other tools to reduce manual work

Document your workflow: Ensure all team members understand how to use Git in your project

Regular maintenance: Periodically clean up old branches, optimize the repository, and review your workflow

Continuous learning: Git and related tools are constantly evolving, so encourage ongoing learning and improvement

Conclusion

Git is more than just a version control system; when used effectively, it becomes an integral part of your project management toolkit. By choosing the right workflow, integrating Git with other project management tools, and following best practices, you can significantly improve your team's productivity and the quality of your codebase.

Chapter 4: Remote Repositories and Collaboration

4.1 Introduction to Remote Repositories

Remote repositories are versions of your project that are hosted on the Internet or network somewhere. Collaborating with others involves managing these remote repositories and pushing and pulling data to and from them when you need to share work.

4.1.1 Why Use Remote Repositories?

Remote repositories serve several crucial purposes:

Collaboration: They allow multiple people to work on the same project.

Backup: They serve as an off-site backup of your project.

Deployment: They can be used as part of a deployment pipeline.

Open Source: They enable you to contribute to open source projects.

4.1.2 Common Hosting Platforms

While you can set up your own Git server, many developers use hosting platforms like:

GitHub

GitLab

Bitbucket

Azure DevOps

These platforms provide additional features like issue tracking, pull requests, and continuous integration/continuous deployment (CI/CD) pipelines.

4.2 Cloning a Remote Repository

Cloning is how you create a local of a remote repository.

4.2.1 Basic Cloning

To clone a repository:

```
git clone https://github.com/username/repository.git
```

This creates a new directory with the repository name, initializes a `.git` directory inside it, pulls down all the data for that repository, and checks out a working of the latest version.

4.2.2 Cloning to a Specific Directory

To clone into a directory with a different name:

```
git clone https://github.com/username/repository.git
mydirectory
```

4.2.3 Cloning a Specific Branch

To clone a specific branch:

```
git         clone         -b         branch-name
https://github.com/username/repository.git
```

4.3 Managing Remote Repositories

Once you've cloned a repository or created a new one, you'll need to manage your remote connections.

4.3.1 Viewing Remote Repositories

To see which remote servers you have configured:

```
git remote
```

To see the URLs that Git has stored for each remote:

```
git remote -v
```

4.3.2 Adding Remote Repositories

To add a new remote repository:

```
git remote add <shortname> <url>
```

For example:

```
git            remote            add            origin
https://github.com/username/new-repository.git
```

4.3.3 Renaming and Removing Remotes

To rename a remote:

```
git remote rename old-name new-name
```

To remove a remote:

```
git remote remove remote-name
```

4.4 Fetching and Pulling from Remotes

Fetching and pulling are how you get data from remote repositories.

4.4.1 Fetching

Fetching downloads new data from a remote repository, but it doesn't integrate any of this new data into your working files:

```
git fetch <remote>
```

For example:

```
git fetch origin
```

4.4.2 Pulling

Pulling is essentially a `git fetch` immediately followed by a `git merge`. It downloads new data and immediately updates your current branch to incorporate the new changes:

93

```
git pull <remote> <branch>
```

For example:

```
git pull origin main
```

4.4.3 Fetch vs. Pull

Use `fetch` when you want to see what others have been working on, without merging those changes into your local branch.

Use `pull` when you want to update your current branch with the latest changes from the remote.

4.5 Pushing to Remotes

Pushing is how you transfer commits from your local repository to a remote repository.

4.5.1 Basic Pushing

To push your changes to a remote repository:

```
git push <remote> <branch>
```

For example:

```
git push origin main
```

4.5.2 Pushing to a New Branch

If you're pushing a local branch for the first time:

```
git push -u origin new-branch
```

The -u flag sets up tracking, which simplifies future push and pull commands for this branch.

4.5.3 Force Pushing

In some cases, you might need to overwrite the remote branch with your local branch:

```
git push --force origin branch-name
```

Warning: Force pushing can overwrite changes on the remote, potentially causing others to lose work. Use with caution, especially on shared branches.

4.6 Working with Forks

Forking is a way of creating a personal of someone else's project. Forks are commonly used in open source development.

4.6.1 Creating a Fork

Most hosting platforms allow you to fork a repository through their web interface.

4.6.2 Cloning Your Fork

After forking, clone your fork to your local machine:

```
git clone https://github.com/your-username/forked-repository.git
```

4.6.3 Keeping Your Fork Updated

To keep your fork updated with the original repository:

Add the original repository as a remote (often called "upstream"):

```
git remote add upstream https://github.com/original-owner/original-repository.git
```

Fetch changes from the upstream repository:

```
git fetch upstream
```

Merge the changes into your local main branch:

```
git checkout main

git merge upstream/main
```

4.7 Collaborative Workflows

Different teams might use different workflows when collaborating with Git. Here are a few common ones:

4.7.1 Centralized Workflow

In this simple workflow, everyone works on the main branch:

Clone the central repository

Make changes locally

Pull to get any new changes

Push your changes

This works for small teams, but can lead to conflicts in larger projects.

4.7.2 Feature Branch Workflow

This workflow revolves around topic branches:

Create a new branch for each feature

Work on the feature in its branch

Open a pull request when the feature is complete

After review, merge the feature branch into main

This workflow is good for most teams as it keeps the main branch clean and allows for code review.

4.7.3 Gitflow Workflow

Gitflow is a robust framework for managing larger projects:

`main` branch stores official release history

`develop` branch serves as an integration branch for features

Feature branches for new features

Release branches for preparing releases

Hotfix branches for quick patches to production

While powerful, Gitflow can be complex for smaller projects.

4.7.4 Forking Workflow

Common in open source projects:

Fork the official repository

Clone your fork locally

Create a feature branch in your local repository

Push your feature branch to your fork

Open a pull request from your fork to the official repository

This workflow is great for open source projects as it doesn't require giving write access to contributors.

4.8 Pull Requests

Pull requests are a way to notify others about changes you've pushed to a branch in a repository. They're a key part of most collaborative workflows.

4.8.1 Creating a Pull Request

Most hosting platforms allow you to create pull requests through their web interface. The general process is:

Push your changes to a branch in your repository

Navigate to your repository on the hosting platform

Click on "Pull requests" and then "New pull request"

Select the branch with your changes as the compare branch

Write a title and description for your pull request

Click "Create pull request"

4.8.2 Reviewing Pull Requests

When reviewing a pull request:

Look at the changes in the "Files changed" tab

Leave comments on specific lines if you have questions or suggestions

Test the changes if possible

Approve the pull request if everything looks good, or request changes if needed

4.8.3 Merging Pull Requests

Once a pull request has been approved:

Click the "Merge pull request" button on the hosting platform

Optionally, delete the feature branch after merging

4.9 Handling Merge Conflicts in Collaborative Settings

Merge conflicts can occur when multiple people make changes to the same parts of a file. Here's how to handle them:

Pull the latest changes from the remote repository

If Git reports a conflict, open the conflicting file(s)

Look for conflict markers (<<<<<<<, =======, >>>>>>>)

Decide which changes to keep

Remove the conflict markers

Stage the resolved files (`git add <filename>`)

Commit the merge (`git commit -m "Resolve merge conflict"`)

Push the changes

Communication with your team is key when resolving conflicts to ensure everyone's work is properly integrated.

4.10 Best Practices for Collaboration

When collaborating with others using Git, keep these best practices in mind:

Communicate: Keep your team informed about what you're working on.

Pull Frequently: Regularly pull changes from the remote to stay up-to-date.

Use Branches: Work on features or fixes in separate branches.

Write Good Commit Messages: Clear, descriptive commit messages help others understand your changes.

Review Code: Use pull requests and code reviews to maintain code quality.

Keep Commits Atomic: Each commit should represent a single logical change.

Don't Rewrite Public History: Avoid force pushing or rewriting history on shared branches.

Use Issues: Use your platform's issue tracker to manage tasks and bugs.

Document: Keep your project's documentation up-to-date.

CI/CD: Implement continuous integration and deployment to catch issues early.

4.11 Troubleshooting Common Issues

Here are some common issues you might encounter when working with remote repositories, and how to solve them:

4.11.1 Permission Denied (publickey)

If you see this error when trying to push or pull, it means Git can't authenticate with the remote server. To fix:

Ensure you have an SSH key set up on your local machine

Add your public key to your account on the hosting platform

Make sure you're using the SSH URL for the repository, not the HTTPS URL

4.11.2 Remote Already Exists

If you try to add a remote that already exists, you'll get an error. To fix:

Use a different name for the new remote, or

Remove the existing remote first: `git remote remove <name>`

4.11.3 Non-Fast-Forward Errors

This occurs when you try to push changes but the remote branch has been updated. To fix:

Pull the latest changes: `git pull origin <branch>`

Resolve any conflicts

Push your changes again

4.11.4 Large File Rejection

If you try to push a file larger than the remote allows, your push will be rejected. To fix:

Remove the large file from your repository

Use Git Large File Storage (LFS) for large files

4.12 Advanced Topics

As you become more comfortable with remote repositories and collaboration, you might want to explore these advanced topics:

4.12.1 Submodules

Submodules allow you to keep a Git repository as a subdirectory of another Git repository. This is useful for including external libraries or shared components.

4.12.2 Git Hooks

Git hooks are scripts that Git executes before or after events such as commit, push, and receive. They can be used to enforce certain workflows or coding standards.

4.12.3 Rebasing vs. Merging

While we covered basic rebasing earlier, understanding when to use rebasing versus merging in a collaborative setting is an advanced topic worth exploring.

4.12.4 Git Attributes

Git attributes allow you to specify separate merge strategies for specific files or directories, apply filters, or exclude files from exports.

4.13 Conclusion

Working with remote repositories and collaborating with others is a fundamental part of using Git in a professional setting. By understanding these concepts and practicing the techniques we've covered, you'll be well-equipped to contribute to projects and work effectively in a team.

Remember, collaboration is as much about communication and teamwork as it is about technical skills. As you work on projects with others, focus on clear communication, good documentation, and following established best practices.

In the next chapter, we'll dive into more advanced Git techniques, building on the foundation we've established in these first four chapters.

Chapter 5: Advanced Git Techniques

Introduction

As you become more proficient with Git, you'll discover that it offers a wealth of advanced features and techniques that can significantly enhance your workflow. This chapter delves into these advanced concepts, providing you with the knowledge to leverage Git's full potential. We'll explore powerful commands, discuss complex scenarios, and introduce you to techniques that can help you manage large projects more effectively. By mastering these advanced techniques, you'll be able to handle even the most challenging version control situations with confidence.

Rewriting History

One of Git's most powerful (and potentially dangerous) features is its ability to rewrite history. This can be incredibly useful for cleaning up your commit history before sharing your work, but it should be used with caution, especially on public branches.

Interactive Rebasing

Interactive rebasing is a powerful tool that allows you to modify commits in many ways. You can reorder, edit, squash, or even delete commits entirely.

To start an interactive rebase, use the following command:

```
git rebase -i <commit>
```

Replace <commit> with the commit hash or reference (like HEAD~3) that you want to start rebasing from.

This will open your default text editor with a list of commits and commands. You can change the command (pick, reword, edit, squash, fixup, drop) for each commit to modify how it's treated during the rebase.

For example, to squash several commits into one:

```
pick f7f3f6d Change button color

squash 310154e Update button padding

squash a5f4a0d Refactor button component
```

This would combine the second and third commits into the first one.

Remember, interactive rebasing rewrites history, so only use it on commits that haven't been pushed to a shared repository.

Commit Amending

Sometimes, you might want to modify your most recent commit. Maybe you forgot to add a file, or you want to change the commit message. The `--amend` flag allows you to do this:

```
git commit --amend
```

This opens your editor to modify the most recent commit message. If you've staged changes, they'll be added to the amended commit.

To add forgotten files without changing the commit message:

```
git add forgotten_file
git commit --amend --no-edit
```

Again, only amend commits that haven't been pushed to a shared repository.

Cherry-Picking

Cherry-picking allows you to apply the changes introduced by some existing commits. This can be useful when you want to pick specific changes from one branch and apply them to another.

To cherry-pick a commit:

```
git cherry-pick <commit-hash>
```

This creates a new commit on your current branch with the changes from the specified commit.

You can cherry-pick multiple commits:

```
git cherry-pick <commit-hash-1> <commit-hash-2>
```

If you just want to apply the changes without creating a new commit, use the `--no-commit` or `-n` flag:

```
git cherry-pick -n <commit-hash>
```

Resetting

The `git reset` command is a powerful tool for undoing changes. It moves the current branch tip backward to a specified commit, essentially rewriting the commit history.

There are three main options for reset:

Soft reset (`--soft`): Moves the HEAD to the specified commit, but leaves the changes in the staging area.

Mixed reset (default): Moves the HEAD and updates the staging area with the contents of the specified commit.

Hard reset (`--hard`): Moves the HEAD, updates the staging area, and updates the working directory to match the specified commit.

For example, to undo the last commit but keep the changes staged:

```
git reset --soft HEAD~1
```

To completely undo the last commit and all changes:

```
git reset --hard HEAD~1
```

Be very careful with `git reset`, especially `--hard`, as it can result in losing work if used incorrectly.

Advanced Branching Techniques

While we covered basic branching in earlier chapters, there are some advanced branching techniques that can be very useful in complex projects.

Orphan Branches

An orphan branch is a branch that starts with no commit history. This can be useful for things like creating a new `gh-pages` branch for GitHub Pages.

To create an orphan branch:

```
git checkout --orphan new-branch
```

This creates a new branch with no parents. The working directory remains unchanged, but none of the files are staged for commit.

Worktrees

Git worktrees allow you to check out multiple branches of the same repository into different directories. This can be useful when you need to work on multiple branches simultaneously.

To add a new worktree:

```
git worktree add ../path-to-new-directory branch-name
```

This checks out the specified branch into a new directory. You can now work on this branch independently of your main working directory.

To list worktrees:

```
git worktree list
```

To remove a worktree:

```
git worktree remove path-to-worktree
```

Reflog

The reflog is a mechanism Git uses to record updates applied to branch tips and other references. It's like a safety net, allowing you to recover lost commits or branches.

To view the reflog:

```
git reflog
```

This shows a log of all reference updates in the repository. You can use this to find lost commits or branches and recover them.

For example, to recover a branch that was accidentally deleted:

```
git checkout -b recovered-branch <sha>
```

Where `<sha>` is the commit hash of the branch tip before it was deleted, found in the reflog.

Submodules and Subtrees

When working on large projects, you might need to include other projects within your project. Git provides two main ways to do this: submodules and subtrees.

Submodules

Submodules allow you to keep a Git repository as a subdirectory of another Git repository. This lets you clone another repository into your project and keep your commits separate.

To add a submodule:

```
git submodule add https://github.com/example/repo.git
path/to/submodule
```

This creates a new directory at the specified path, clones the repository there, and adds it as a submodule.

When cloning a project with submodules, you need to initialize and update them:

```
git submodule init

git submodule update
```

Or, you can clone with submodules in one command:

```
git          clone            --recurse-submodules
https://github.com/example/repo.git
```

Submodules can be tricky to work with, as they point to a specific commit in the submodule's repository. When you want to update a submodule to a newer version:

```
cd path/to/submodule
```

```
git fetch

git checkout master

git pull

cd ../..

git add path/to/submodule

git commit -m "Update submodule to latest"
```

Subtrees

Subtrees are an alternative to submodules. They allow you to insert another project into a subdirectory of your main project.

To add a subtree:

```
git    subtree    add    --prefix=path/to/subtree
https://github.com/example/repo.git master --squash
```

This adds the `master` branch of the specified repository as a subtree in the specified path.

To update a subtree:

```
git    subtree    pull    --prefix=path/to/subtree
https://github.com/example/repo.git master --squash
```

Subtrees are generally easier to use than submodules, as they don't require special commands to clone or update.

However, they can make your repository larger, as the entire history of the subtree is included in your main repository.

Git Hooks

Git hooks are scripts that Git executes before or after events such as: commit, push, and receive. They can be used to enforce certain workflows, automatically run tests, or perform custom actions at specific points in your Git workflow.

Hook scripts are stored in the `.git/hooks` directory of your Git repository. To enable a hook, rename the sample file (removing the .sample extension) and make it executable.

Some common hooks include:

`pre-commit`: Runs before a commit is created. Can be used to run tests or lint code.

`prepare-commit-msg`: Runs after the default commit message is created but before the commit message editor is started.

`post-commit`: Runs after a commit is created. Can be used for notifications.

`pre-push`: Runs before a push is started. Can be used to run tests or prevent pushing to certain branches.

Here's an example of a simple `pre-commit` hook that runs tests before allowing a commit:

bash

```
#!/bin/sh


npm test


# $? stores exit value of the last command

if [ $? -ne 0 ]; then

echo "Tests must pass before commit!"

exit 1

fi
```

Remember, hooks are not transferred with `git clone` of a project. You'll need to distribute them manually or include them in your project files (outside of `.git`) with instructions for installation.

Advanced Merging Techniques

While we covered basic merging in earlier chapters, there are some advanced merging techniques that can be useful in complex situations.

Merge Strategies

Git has several merge strategies available. The default is usually the "recursive" strategy, but you can specify others:

`ours`: Forces conflicting hunks to be auto-resolved cleanly by favoring the current branch version.

`theirs`: The opposite of `ours`, favors the version being merged in.

`octopus`: Can merge multiple branches at once.

To use a specific merge strategy:

```
git merge -s <strategy> <branch>
```

Merge Options

You can also pass options to the merge command to change its behavior:

`--no-ff`: Always create a merge commit, even if a fast-forward is possible.

`--squash`: Squash all commits from the merging branch into a single commit.

`-X ignore-space-change`: Ignore whitespace changes when resolving conflicts.

For example:

116

```
git merge --no-ff feature-branch
```

Resolving Complex Merge Conflicts

Sometimes, you'll encounter complex merge conflicts that aren't easily resolved. Here are some techniques to handle these:

Use `git mergetool`: This opens a visual diff tool to help resolve conflicts.

Use `git checkout --ours` or `git checkout --theirs` to choose one version over another for a specific file.

Use `git log --merge` to see commits that touched a file with merge conflicts.

Remember, communication with your team is crucial when resolving complex merge conflicts to ensure everyone's work is properly integrated.

Git Internals

Understanding Git's internals can help you use Git more effectively and troubleshoot issues when they arise.

Git Objects

Git's object model is based on four types of objects:

Blobs: Store file data

Trees: Store directory structures

Commits: Store commit information

Tags: Store annotated tag information

You can inspect these objects using the `git cat-file` command:

```
git cat-file -p <object-hash>
```

The Git Index

The index (or staging area) is a binary file in the .git directory that stores a snapshot of your working tree. When you run `git add`, you're updating the index.

You can view the contents of the index with:

```
git ls-files --stage
```

Packfiles

Git periodically packs many loose objects into a single binary file called a packfile to save space and be more efficient. You can manually trigger this with:

```
git gc
```

Understanding these internals can help you debug issues and understand what's happening "under the hood" when you run Git commands.

Customizing Git

Git allows for extensive customization to fit your workflow.

Git Config

You can configure Git at three levels: system, global (user), and local (repository). Some useful configurations:

```
git config --global alias.co checkout

git config --global core.editor vim

git config --global merge.tool kdiff3
```

Git Attributes

Git attributes allow you to specify different merge strategies, diff algorithms, or filters for specific files or directories. These are set in a .gitattributes file.

For example, to always use the ours merge strategy for a specific file:

```
database.xml merge=ours
```

Creating Custom Git Commands

You can create custom Git commands by creating scripts named `git-<command>` in your PATH. For example, a script named `git-hello` would be invoked with `git hello`.

Performance Optimization

As your Git repository grows, you might need to optimize its performance.

Shallow Clones

If you only need the recent history of a large repository, you can create a shallow clone:

```
git clone --depth 1 <repository-url>
```

This clones only the most recent commit.

Partial Clones

Git 2.17 introduced partial clones, which allow you to clone a repository without downloading all the blob objects:

```
git clone --filter=blob:none <repository-url>
```

Git LFS (Large File Storage)

For repositories with large files, Git LFS can significantly improve performance. It replaces large files with text pointers inside Git, while storing the file contents on a remote server.

To use Git LFS:

```
git lfs install

git lfs track "*.psd"
```

Debugging with Git

Git provides several tools to help with debugging.

Git Bisect

`git bisect` helps you find the commit that introduced a bug using a binary search.

To start a bisect:

```
git bisect start

git bisect bad  # Current version is bad

git bisect good <known-good-commit>
```

Git will then checkout commits, and you tell it whether each one is good or bad until it finds the first bad commit.

Git Blame

`git blame` shows you which commit last modified each line of a file:

```
git blame filename
```

This can be useful for understanding the context of changes.

Git Grep

`git grep` allows you to search for a string or regular expression in any committed version of your project:

```
git grep "TODO" $(git rev-list --all)
```

This searches for "TODO" in all commits.

Working with Large Repositories

When working with large repositories, you might encounter some unique challenges.

Handling Large Files

As mentioned earlier, Git LFS is a good solution for handling large files. Another option is to use `git sparse-checkout`, which allows you to checkout only part of your repository:

```
git sparse-checkout set <directory>
```

Managing Many Branches

When dealing with many branches, you can use `git branch --merged` and `git branch --no-merged` to see which branches have or haven't been merged into the current branch.

To delete all merged branches:

```
git branch --merged | grep -v "\*" | xargs -n 1 git branch -d
```

Cleaning Up Old Commits

The `git filter-branch` command allows you to rewrite a large number of commits according to certain patterns. For example, to remove a file from the entire history:

```
git filter-branch --tree-filter 'rm -f passwords.txt' HEAD
```

Be very careful with this command, as it rewrites history.

Git in Continuous Integration/Continuous Deployment (CI/CD)

Git plays a crucial role in modern CI/CD pipelines.

Git Hooks in CI/CD

You can use Git hooks to trigger CI/CD pipelines. For example, a `post-receive` hook on your Git server could trigger a deployment when changes are pushed.

Git in Jenkins

Jenkins, a popular CI/CD tool, can poll Git repositories for changes or be triggered by Git hooks. You can configure Jenkins to checkout specific branches, tags, or even use Git parameters in your builds.

GitHub Actions

GitHub Actions allow you to create custom workflows triggered by Git events. For example, you could create a workflow that runs tests on every push to a branch:

yaml

```
on: [push]

jobs:

test:

runs-on: ubuntu-latest

steps:

uses: actions/checkout@v2

name: Run tests

run: npm test
```

Git Best Practices

As we conclude this chapter on advanced Git techniques, let's review some best practices:

Keep commits atomic: Each commit should represent a single logical change.

Write good commit messages: Use the imperative mood and explain why the change was made.

Use branches liberally: Create a new branch for each feature or bug fix.

Pull frequently: Keep your local repository up-to-date to minimize merge conflicts.

Don't rewrite public history: Avoid using force push or rebase on shared branches.

Use tags for releases: Create

Chapter 6: Git Workflows and Project Management

Introduction

In the previous chapters, we've explored the technical aspects of Git, from basic commands to advanced techniques. Now, we'll shift our focus to how Git is used in real-world scenarios, particularly in the context of project management and team collaboration. This chapter will delve into various Git workflows, discuss how to integrate Git with project management methodologies, and explore best practices for using Git in large-scale projects.

Understanding Git Workflows

A Git workflow is a recipe or recommendation for how to use Git to accomplish work in a consistent and productive manner. Git workflows encourage developers and DevOps teams to leverage Git effectively and consistently. Git offers a lot of flexibility in how users manage changes, and several workflows have emerged as best practices depending on the size of the team, the project, and the deployment model.

The Centralized Workflow

The Centralized Workflow is the simplest of all workflows and is often the starting point for teams transitioning from SVN. In this model:

There is a single "central" repository.

Developers clone the central repository, make changes locally, and push their new commits directly back to the central repository.

There is only one main branch, often called "master" or "main".

This workflow works well for small teams or projects with few conflicts. However, it can lead to problems when multiple developers try to push changes to the same branch simultaneously.

Pros:

Simple to understand and implement

Works well for small teams or projects

Cons:

Can lead to conflicts in busy repositories

Lacks isolation for new features or experiments

Feature Branch Workflow

The Feature Branch Workflow builds on the Centralized Workflow by requiring developers to create a new branch for each feature or fix. This approach:

Keeps the main branch clean and always deployable

Makes it easier to conduct code reviews via pull requests

Allows for experimentation without affecting the main codebase

In this workflow:

Developers create a new branch for each feature or bug fix

Work is done on these feature branches

When complete, the developer opens a pull request

After code review and any necessary changes, the feature branch is merged into the main branch

This workflow is popular because it strikes a balance between simplicity and isolation of work.

Pros:

Keeps the main branch clean

Facilitates code reviews

Allows for experimentation

Cons:

Can lead to long-lived branches if not managed properly

May require more Git knowledge from team members

Gitflow Workflow

The Gitflow Workflow is a robust framework for managing larger projects. Gitflow defines a strict branching model designed around the project release. It assigns very specific roles to different branches and defines how and when they should interact.

In Gitflow:

The 'master' branch stores the official release history

A parallel 'develop' branch serves as an integration branch for features

Feature branches are used for new features and bug fixes

Release branches prepare new production releases

Hotfix branches allow for emergency fixes to production releases

While powerful, Gitflow can be complex and may be overkill for smaller projects or teams practicing continuous delivery.

Pros:

Provides a robust framework for managing releases

Well-suited for projects with a scheduled release cycle

Allows for parallel development of multiple features

Cons:

Can be complex to understand and implement

May introduce unnecessary overhead for smaller projects

Can lead to merge conflicts in long-lived branches

Forking Workflow

The Forking Workflow is fundamentally different from the other workflows. Instead of using a single server-side repository to act as the "central" codebase, it gives every developer their own server-side repository. This means that each contributor has not one, but two Git repositories: a private local one and a public server-side one.

The main steps in a Forking Workflow are:

A developer 'forks' an 'official' server-side repository, creating their own server-side

The new server-side is cloned to their local system

A Git remote path for the 'official' repository is added to the local clone

A new local feature branch is created

The developer makes changes on the new branch

New commits are pushed to their own public repository

The developer opens a pull request from the new branch to the 'official' repository

The pull request gets approved and merged by the project maintainer

This workflow is often seen in open source projects, as it allows contributions from developers who may not have push access to the main repository.

Pros:

Allows for contributions from a wide range of developers

Provides a clear separation between the official codebase and contributor's work

Reduces the need for complex permission management on the main repository

Cons:

Can be complex to set up and manage

May lead to divergence if the main repository changes rapidly

Requires more Git operations for simple changes

Trunk-Based Development

Trunk-Based Development is a source-control branching model where developers collaborate on code in a single branch called 'trunk', resist any pressure to create other long-lived development branches, and therefore avoid merge hell, do not break the build, and live happily ever after.

Key aspects of Trunk-Based Development include:

Short-lived feature branches, if used at all

Developers integrate their work to the trunk at least once a day

High reliance on feature toggles and other techniques to keep the trunk always releasable

Emphasis on automated testing and continuous integration

This approach is gaining popularity, especially in teams practicing continuous delivery or continuous deployment.

Pros:

Simplifies the development process

Reduces merge conflicts and integration problems

Facilitates continuous integration and delivery

Cons:

Requires a high level of discipline from the development team

May be challenging for less experienced Git users

Can be difficult to implement in larger teams or more complex projects

Choosing the Right Workflow

Selecting the right Git workflow depends on several factors:

Team size and structure

Project complexity

Release schedule

Deployment model (e.g., continuous delivery vs. scheduled releases)

Team's Git expertise

It's important to remember that these workflows are not mutually exclusive, and many teams use hybrid approaches that combine elements from different workflows. The key is to find a workflow that enhances your team's productivity and suits your project's needs.

Integrating Git with Project Management

Git isn't just a version control system; when used effectively, it can be a powerful tool for project management. Here are some ways to integrate Git into your project management practices:

Issue Tracking

Many Git hosting platforms (like GitHub, GitLab, and Bitbucket) provide built-in issue tracking. You can link issues to specific commits, branches, or pull requests. This creates a clear connection between the problem, the solution, and the code changes.

Best practices for issue tracking with Git:

Use a consistent naming convention for branches that includes the issue number (e.g., `feature/123-add-login-page`)

Reference issue numbers in commit messages (e.g., "Fix login bug #456")

Use keywords in pull request descriptions to automatically close issues when merged (e.g., "Closes #789")

Project Boards

Project boards (like GitHub Projects or GitLab Boards) allow you to create Kanban-style boards directly linked to your Git repository. You can move issues and pull requests through columns representing different stages of your workflow.

Tips for using project boards:

Create columns that match your development process (e.g., To Do, In Progress, Review, Done)

Use automation to move cards based on Git events (e.g., move to 'Review' when a pull request is opened)

Use labels to categorize and filter issues and pull requests

Milestones

Milestones allow you to group issues and pull requests into broader goals or releases. You can set due dates for milestones and track progress towards completion.

Effective use of milestones:

Create a milestone for each planned release or sprint

Assign relevant issues and pull requests to the milestone

Use the milestone's progress bar to track completion

Code Reviews

Pull requests facilitate code reviews, an essential part of many development workflows. Good code review practices can improve code quality, share knowledge, and catch bugs early.

Code review best practices:

Keep pull requests small and focused

Use pull request templates to ensure all necessary information is provided

Automate checks (e.g., linting, tests) to run on pull requests

Encourage constructive and respectful feedback

Continuous Integration/Continuous Deployment (CI/CD)

Git can be tightly integrated with CI/CD pipelines. Many CI/CD tools can be triggered by Git events (like pushes or pull requests) and can update the status of commits or pull requests based on build and test results.

CI/CD integration tips:

Set up automated tests to run on every push

Use branch protection rules to require passing CI checks before merging

Automate deployments based on Git events (e.g., deploy to staging when merged to develop, deploy to production when tagged)

Documentation

Git repositories aren't just for code. They're also excellent places to store and version control documentation. Many teams use markdown files in their Git repositories for documentation, which can be automatically rendered on platforms like GitHub or GitLab.

Documentation best practices:

Keep a README.md file in the root of your repository with essential project information

Use a docs/ directory for more detailed documentation

Consider using GitHub Pages or similar tools to publish documentation directly from your repository

Git for Large-Scale Projects

As projects grow in size and complexity, effectively using Git becomes more challenging. Here are some strategies for managing Git in large-scale projects:

Monorepo vs. Multirepo

One of the first decisions for large projects is whether to use a monorepo (one large repository for all code) or a multirepo (multiple smaller repositories) approach.

Monorepo pros:

Easier to manage dependencies and share code

Simplified CI/CD setup

Easier to refactor across project boundaries

Monorepo cons:

Can become very large, leading to slow clones and operations

May require specialized tools to manage

Can be overwhelming for new team members

Multirepo pros:

Clearer ownership and access control

Faster Git operations on individual repositories

Easier to understand for new team members

Multirepo cons:

More complex dependency management

More challenging to make cross-cutting changes

May lead to code duplication

Managing Large Repositories

If you're working with a large repository:

Use shallow clones (`git clone --depth 1`) for faster initial clones

Use Git LFS (Large File Storage) for large binary files

Regularly clean up old branches and use `git gc` to optimize the repository

Branch Management

In large projects, branch management becomes crucial:

Use a clear naming convention for branches (e.g., `feature/`, `bugfix/`, `hotfix/`)

Regularly delete merged branches

Consider using tools like GitLab's "merge when pipeline succeeds" feature to manage busy branches

Code Organization

Organize your code in a way that makes sense for your project:

Use clear, consistent directory structures

Consider using Git submodules or subtrees for shared components

Use .gitignore files effectively to exclude unnecessary files

Team Structure

For large teams:

Use CODEOWNERS files to automatically request reviews from the right people

Consider using GitHub's "required reviewers" feature

Use teams and roles in your Git hosting platform to manage permissions

Git Best Practices for Project Management

To wrap up, here are some overall best practices for using Git in project management:

Commit often: Make small, frequent commits rather than large, infrequent ones

Write clear commit messages: Use a consistent format and provide context

Use branches effectively: Create a new branch for each feature or bug fix

Keep the main branch stable: Only merge thoroughly tested code into the main branch

Automate where possible: Use CI/CD, automated tests, and other tools to reduce manual work

Document your workflow: Ensure all team members understand how to use Git in your project

Regular maintenance: Periodically clean up old branches, optimize the repository, and review your workflow

Continuous learning: Git and related tools are constantly evolving, so encourage ongoing learning and improvement

Conclusion

Git is more than just a version control system; when used effectively, it becomes an integral part of your project management toolkit. By choosing the right workflow, integrating Git with other project management tools, and following best practices, you can significantly improve your team's productivity and the quality of your codebase.

Remember, the "right" way to use Git will depend on your specific project and team. Don't be afraid to experiment with different approaches and adapt your workflow as your project evolves. The key is to find a system that works for your team and helps you deliver high-quality software efficiently.

In the next chapter, we'll explore how to troubleshoot common Git problems and recover from mistakes, further enhancing your Git mastery.

Chapter 7: Troubleshooting and Recovering from Mistakes in Git

Introduction

Even the most experienced Git users make mistakes or encounter issues. The good news is that Git is designed with safety and recoverability in mind. In this chapter, we'll explore common Git problems, how to troubleshoot them, and most importantly, how to recover from mistakes. We'll cover scenarios ranging from simple commit message typos to more complex situations like lost commits or corrupted repositories.

Remember, one of Git's strengths is that it's very difficult to truly lose work once it's been committed. With the right knowledge and tools, you can recover from almost any situation.

Common Git Issues and Their Solutions

Let's start by addressing some of the most common issues Git users encounter and how to resolve them.

Fixing Commit Messages

Scenario: You've just made a commit but realized there's a typo in the commit message.

Solution: Use the --amend flag with `git commit`:

```
git commit --amend
```

This opens your default editor, allowing you to modify the most recent commit message. If you don't need to edit the message in an editor, you can use:

```
git commit --amend -m "New commit message"
```

Remember, only amend commits that haven't been pushed to a shared repository, as this rewrites history.

Unstaging a File

Scenario: You've accidentally staged a file that you don't want to include in the next commit.

Solution: Use `git reset`:

```
git reset HEAD <file>
```

This unstages the file but keeps your changes in the working directory.

Unmodifying a Modified File

144

Scenario: You've made changes to a file but want to revert it to the state it was in the last commit.

Solution: Use `git checkout`:

```
git checkout -- <file>
```

Be careful with this command, as it discards your changes in the working directory.

Recover Deleted Branch

Scenario: You've accidentally deleted a branch that contained important work.

Solution: If the branch was recently deleted, you can often recover it using the reflog:

```
git reflog
```

Find the SHA-1 of the last commit on the deleted branch, then:

```
git branch <branch-name> <sha>
```

Undo a Merge

Scenario: You've merged a branch but immediately realized it was a mistake.

Solution: If you haven't pushed the merge, you can reset to the commit before the merge:

```
git reset --hard HEAD~1
```

If you have pushed the merge, it's better to revert the merge:

```
git revert -m 1 <merge-commit-sha>
```

Recover Lost Commits

Scenario: You've lost some commits, perhaps due to a hard reset or a deleted branch.

Solution: The reflog is your friend here:

```
git reflog
```

Find the SHA-1 of the lost commit, then you can create a new branch at that commit:

```
git branch recovery-branch <sha>
```

Resolve Merge Conflicts

Scenario: You're merging or rebasing and encounter merge conflicts.

Solution:

Open the conflicting files and look for conflict markers
(<<<<<<<, =======, >>>>>>>).

Edit the files to resolve the conflicts, removing the
conflict markers.

Stage the resolved files: `git add <resolved-files>`

Complete the merge or rebase:

For a merge: `git commit`

For a rebase: `git rebase --continue`

Advanced Troubleshooting and Recovery

Now let's look at some more complex scenarios and how to
handle them.

Recovering from a Corrupted Repository

Scenario: Your repository seems to be in a corrupted state,
with Git operations failing.

Solution: First, try running Git's built-in filesystem check:

```
git fsck
```

This will report any corrupt objects. If corruption is found, you may need to use more advanced recovery techniques:

Try to repair the repository:

```
git gc --auto
git repack -d -l
```

If that doesn't work, you might need to clone the repository fresh and manually over your recent (uncommitted) work.

Retrieving Lost Data with Git Objects

Scenario: You've lost some work and can't find it in the reflog.

Solution: Git keeps all objects for some time, even if they're not referenced by any branch or tag. You can find these objects:

Use `git fsck` to find dangling objects:

```
git fsck --full --no-reflogs --unreachable --lost-found
```

Examine the contents of dangling blobs or commits:

```
git show <object-sha>
```

If you find your lost work, you can recover it by creating a new branch:

```
git branch recovered-work <object-sha>
```

Recovering from an Accidental Git Reset

Scenario: You've accidentally run `git reset --hard` and lost commits.

Solution: The reflog can help here too:

Check the reflog:

```
git reflog
```

Find the SHA-1 of the commit you reset from.

Reset back to that commit:

```
git reset --hard <sha>
```

Fixing a Detached HEAD State

Scenario: You find yourself in a "detached HEAD" state.

Solution: If you want to keep the work you've done in this state:

Create a new branch where you are:

```
git branch temp
```

Switch to the new branch:

```
git checkout temp
```

If you don't want to keep the work, simply checkout an existing branch:

```
git checkout main
```

Recovering from a Failed Rebase

Scenario: You're in the middle of a rebase that's gone wrong.

Solution: You have a few options:

To abort the rebase and return to the state before you started:

```
git rebase --abort
```

To skip the current commit and continue with the next:

```
git rebase --skip
```

To manually fix conflicts, edit the files, stage them, and then:

```
git rebase --continue
```

Undoing a Published Rebase

Scenario: You've rebased and force-pushed a shared branch, causing issues for your team.

Solution: This is a tricky situation, as it rewrites public history. The best approach is often:

Communicate with your team to ensure everyone is aware of the situation.

Have team members stash their work: `git stash`

Reset the branch back to its state on the remote before the rebase:

```
git fetch origin

git checkout <branch>

git reset --hard origin/<branch>
```

Reapply the rebase more carefully, or merge instead.

Force-push the corrected history: `git push --force-with-lease`

Have team members pull the corrected history and reapply their stashed work.

Recovering Deleted Files

Scenario: You've accidentally deleted a file and it's not in your latest commit.

Solution: If the file was tracked by Git, you can recover it:

Find the last commit that affected the file:

```
git rev-list -n 1 HEAD -- <file-path>
```

Checkout that version of the file:

```
git checkout <deleting-commit>^ -- <file-path>
```

Fixing Commits Made to the Wrong Branch

Scenario: You've made commits to the wrong branch.

Solution: You can move the commits to the correct branch:

Create a new branch at the current location:

```
git branch newbranch
```

Reset the current branch to before the wrong commits:

```
git reset --hard <sha-before-wrong-commits>
```

Checkout the new branch with the commits:

```
git checkout newbranch
```

Recover from Pushing Sensitive Data

Scenario: You've accidentally pushed sensitive data (like passwords or API keys) to a public repository.

Solution: Removing sensitive data from Git history is complex and should be done carefully:

Use a tool like BFG Repo-Cleaner or `git filter-branch` to remove the sensitive data from the entire Git history.

Force-push the cleaned history to all branches.

Request that all contributors rebase their work onto the new, cleaned history.

Report the security breach if necessary and invalidate/change any exposed credentials.

Remember, even after doing this, the sensitive data may still be cached on Git hosting sites or cloned by others. Always treat exposed credentials as compromised.

Best Practices to Avoid Common Mistakes

While knowing how to recover from mistakes is crucial, it's even better to avoid them in the first place. Here are some best practices:

Use Git Hooks

Git hooks can run scripts before certain Git actions, allowing you to set up safeguards:

Use a pre-commit hook to run tests or linters before allowing a commit.

Use a pre-push hook to prevent pushing directly to protected branches.

Example pre-push hook to prevent pushing to main:

bash

```
#!/bin/sh


protected_branch='main'

current_branch=$(git symbolic-ref HEAD | sed -e
's,.*/\(.*\),\1,')
```

```
if [ $protected_branch = $current_branch ]

then

echo "Direct pushes to $protected_branch are not
allowed. Please use a pull request."

exit 1

fi

exit 0
```

Aliases for Safety

Set up aliases for potentially dangerous commands to
include safeguards:

```
git config --global alias.pushf "push --force-with-
lease"
```

This alias uses `--force-with-lease` instead of `--force`,
which is safer as it checks if the remote branch has been
updated.

Regular Backups

Regularly push your work to a remote repository. This
provides a backup and makes it easier to recover from local
mistakes.

Use a GUI

While command-line Git is powerful, a good GUI can help visualize your repository's state and prevent mistakes. Popular options include:

GitKraken

Sourcetree

GitHub Desktop

Commit Often

Make small, frequent commits. This creates more recovery points and makes it easier to understand and revert changes if needed.

Use Feature Branches

Work on features or fixes in separate branches. This isolates changes and makes it easier to discard or modify work without affecting the main branch.

Code Review

Implement a code review process using pull/merge requests. This provides an extra set of eyes to catch mistakes before they make it into the main branch.

Continuous Integration

Use CI tools to automatically run tests on every push. This can catch issues early and prevent problematic code from being merged.

Understanding Git's Safety Mechanisms

Git has several built-in safety mechanisms that can help you avoid or recover from mistakes:

The Index (Staging Area)

The staging area acts as a buffer between your working directory and the repository. It allows you to carefully craft your commits, reducing the chance of committing unintended changes.

Reflog

The reflog is a log of all ref updates in the repository. It's a powerful tool for recovering lost work. Git keeps the reflog for 90 days by default.

Objects and References

Git's object model means that once data is committed, it's very difficult to truly lose. Even if you can't see it in the current branch structure, the data often still exists in the object database.

Remote Repositories

By regularly pushing to a remote repository, you create a backup of your work. This can be invaluable if your local repository becomes corrupted or lost.

Conclusion

While Git is a powerful tool, it's also a complex one, and mistakes can happen. The key is to understand Git's model and the tools it provides for recovery. Remember these key points:

Git is designed with safety in mind. It's very difficult to truly lose committed work.

The reflog is your best friend for recovering from many types of mistakes.

When in doubt, make a backup. You can always create a new branch to experiment with recovery options.

For complex recovery scenarios, don't hesitate to seek help from more experienced Git users.

Prevention is better than cure. Use best practices and safety measures to avoid common mistakes.

With the knowledge from this chapter, you should be well-equipped to handle most Git troubleshooting scenarios. Remember, every mistake is a learning opportunity. As you encounter and resolve issues, you'll become more proficient with Git and more confident in your ability to manage complex version control scenarios.

In the next chapter, we'll explore advanced Git techniques and workflows, building on the solid foundation we've established throughout this book.

Chapter 8: Advanced Git Techniques and Integrations

Introduction

As we near the end of our journey through Git, it's time to explore some of the more advanced features and techniques that Git offers. We'll also look at how Git can be integrated with other tools and workflows to enhance your development process. This chapter is designed for those who are already comfortable with Git basics and are looking to take their skills to the next level.

Advanced Git Commands and Features

Git Rerere (Reuse Recorded Resolution)

Git Rerere is a powerful feature that allows Git to remember how you've resolved a hunk conflict so that the next time it sees the same conflict, Git can automatically resolve it for you.

To enable Git Rerere:

```
git config --global rerere.enabled true
```

This is particularly useful when you're rebasing a long feature branch, or when you're maintaining a backport branch.

Git Submodules vs Git Subtrees

Both Git Submodules and Git Subtrees allow you to include other Git repositories within your main repository, but they work in different ways.

Git Submodules:

Submodules are pointers to specific commits in other repositories.

They're useful when you want to include another project without incorporating its entire history.

To add a submodule:

```
git submodule add https://github.com/example/repo.git
path/to/submodule
```

Git Subtrees:

Subtrees merge the entire history of another project into a subdirectory of your main project.

They're useful when you want to include another project and have full control over its contents.

To add a subtree:

```
git     subtree     add     --prefix=path/to/subtree
https://github.com/example/repo.git master --squash
```

Git Worktree

Git Worktree allows you to check out multiple branches of
the same repository into different directories. This is useful
when you need to work on multiple features simultaneously
without stashing or committing half-done work.

To create a new worktree:

```
git worktree add ../path-to-new-worktree branch-name
```

Git Bisect

Git Bisect is a powerful debugging tool that uses binary
search to find the commit that introduced a bug.

To start a bisect:

```
git bisect start

git bisect bad  # Current version is bad

git bisect good v1.0  # v1.0 is known to be good
```

Git will then checkout commits in between, and you tell it
whether each one is good or bad until it finds the first bad
commit.

Git Rebase Interactive

Interactive rebase allows you to modify commits in many ways as you move them to the new base. This is a powerful tool for cleaning up your commit history before merging or pushing.

To start an interactive rebase:

```
git rebase -i HEAD~3  # Rebase the last 3 commits
```

This opens an editor where you can mark commits to be picked, edited, squashed, or dropped.

Git Refspec

Refspecs are how Git translates between remote and local branch names. Understanding refspecs can give you fine-grained control over which branches are pushed or pulled.

A refspec is typically of the form:

```
<src>:<dst>
```

For example, to push your local `main` branch to a remote branch named `production`:

```
git push origin main:production
```

Git Notes

Git Notes allow you to add or inspect object annotations without changing the objects themselves. This can be useful for adding metadata to commits without changing their SHA-1.

To add a note:

```
git notes add -m "This is a note" commit-hash
```

To show notes:

```
git log --show-notes
```

Git Customization and Configuration

Git Attributes

Git attributes allow you to specify files or patterns and properties associated with them. This can be used to specify merge strategies, diff algorithms, or filters for specific files.

For example, in your `.gitattributes` file:

```
*.txt diff=text
*.jpg diff=exif
```

This tells Git to use the "text" diff algorithm for .txt files and the "exif" algorithm for .jpg files.

Git Hooks

Git hooks are scripts that Git executes before or after events such as: commit, push, and receive. They can be used to enforce certain workflows, automatic testing, or linting.

Some useful hooks include:

pre-commit: Run tests before allowing a commit

prepare-commit-msg: Modify default commit messages

post-receive: Trigger deployments after receiving a push

Here's a simple pre-commit hook that runs tests:

bash

```
#!/bin/sh

npm test



if [ $? -ne 0 ]; then

echo "Tests must pass before commit!"

exit 1
```

```
fi
```

Custom Git Commands

You can create custom Git commands by creating a script named `git-<command>` in your PATH. For example, a script named `git-hello` would be invoked with `git hello`.

Here's a simple custom command that shows the current branch and status:

```
bash
```

```sh
#!/bin/sh

echo "Current branch: $(git rev-parse --abbrev-ref HEAD)"

git status -s
```

Git for Large Projects

Git Large File Storage (LFS)

Git LFS is an extension that replaces large files with text pointers inside Git, while storing the file contents on a remote server. This can significantly reduce the size of your repository.

To use Git LFS:

```
git lfs install
```

```
git lfs track "*.psd"

git add .gitattributes
```

Partial Clone and Shallow Clone

For large repositories, you can use partial or shallow clones
to reduce the amount of data transferred.

Shallow clone (limited history):

```
git              clone         --depth          1
https://github.com/example/repo.git
```

Partial clone (exclude certain files):

```
git              clone              --filter=blob:none
https://github.com/example/repo.git
```

Sparse Checkout

Sparse checkout allows you to checkout only part of your
repository. This is useful for monorepos or when you only
need a subset of a large project.

To use sparse checkout:

```
git              clone              --no-checkout
https://github.com/example/repo.git

cd repo
```

```
git sparse-checkout init --cone

git sparse-checkout set path/to/directory

git checkout
```

Git Internals

Understanding Git internals can help you use Git more effectively and troubleshoot issues when they arise.

Git Objects

Git's object model is based on four types of objects:

Blobs: Store file data

Trees: Store directory structures

Commits: Store commit information

Tags: Store annotated tag information

You can inspect these objects using the `git cat-file` command:

```
git cat-file -p <object-hash>
```

The Git Index

The index (or staging area) is a binary file in the .git directory that stores a snapshot of your working tree. When you run `git add`, you're updating the index.

You can view the contents of the index with:

```
git ls-files --stage
```

Packfiles

Git periodically packs many loose objects into a single binary file called a packfile to save space and be more efficient. You can manually trigger this with:

```
git gc
```

Integrating Git with Other Tools

Continuous Integration/Continuous Deployment (CI/CD)

Git can be tightly integrated with CI/CD pipelines. Many CI/CD tools can be triggered by Git events and can update the status of commits or pull requests.

For example, with GitHub Actions, you can create a workflow that runs tests on every push:

yaml

```
name: Run Tests

on: [push]
```

```
jobs:

test:

runs-on: ubuntu-latest

steps:

uses: actions/checkout@v2

name: Run tests

run: npm test
```

Issue Tracking

Many Git hosting platforms provide integrated issue tracking. You can link issues to commits, branches, or pull requests.

For example, in GitHub, you can close an issue from a commit message:

```
Fix bug #123
```

Code Review

Git platforms often provide built-in code review tools. For example, GitHub's pull requests or GitLab's merge requests.

To create a pull request in GitHub:

```
git push origin feature-branch
```

Then navigate to your repository on GitHub and click "New pull request".

Project Management Tools

Git can be integrated with various project management tools. For example, Jira has a Git integration that allows you to see commits, branches, and pull requests associated with Jira issues.

To link a commit to a Jira issue, include the issue key in your commit message:

```
git commit -m "PROJ-123 Implement new feature"
```

IDE Integration

Most modern IDEs have built-in Git support or plugins available. For example, Visual Studio Code has excellent Git integration out of the box, allowing you to stage, commit, push, and pull directly from the IDE.

Chat Ops

Chat Ops involves executing commands and viewing their output via chat messages. Many chat platforms can integrate with Git to allow operations like deploying code or checking build status directly from chat.

For example, with Slack and GitHub integration, you might be able to deploy code with a command like:

Advanced Git Workflows

Gitflow

Gitflow is a branching model that defines a strict branching structure designed around project releases. It involves these main branches:

`master`: stores the official release history

`develop`: serves as an integration branch for features

`feature/*`: for developing new features

`release/*`: for preparing releases

`hotfix/*`: for quickly patching production releases

Trunk-Based Development

Trunk-Based Development is a source-control branching model where developers collaborate on code in a single branch called 'trunk', resist any pressure to create other long-lived development branches, and therefore avoid merge hell, do not break the build, and live happily ever after.

Feature Flags

Feature flags (also known as feature toggles) are a powerful technique that allows teams to modify system behavior without changing code. They allow you to enable or disable features at runtime, which can be particularly useful when practicing trunk-based development.

Here's a simple example in JavaScript:

javascript

```javascript
if (featureFlags.newFeature) {
// New feature code

} else {

// Old feature code

}
```

Monorepo vs Polyrepo

A monorepo is a version control repository that stores all of a company's or project's code and assets. A polyrepo approach uses multiple repositories.

Monorepo pros:

Easier to manage dependencies and share code

Simplified CI/CD setup

Easier to refactor across project boundaries

Polyrepo pros:

Clearer ownership and access control

Faster Git operations on individual repositories

Easier to understand for new team members

Git Security Best Practices

Signing Commits

Signing commits cryptographically verifies that commits came from a trusted source. To set up commit signing:

```
git config --global user.signingkey <your-key-id>
git config --global commit.gpgsign true
```

Then to sign a commit:

```
git commit -S -m "Signed commit message"
```

Protected Branches

Most Git hosting platforms allow you to set up protected branches. These branches have restrictions on how changes can be made to them. For example, you might require pull requests and code reviews before merging to the main branch.

Secrets Management

Never commit secrets (like API keys or passwords) to your Git repository. Instead, use environment variables or a secrets management tool.

If you accidentally commit a secret, consider it compromised. Rotate the secret and use a tool like BFG Repo-Cleaner to remove it from your Git history.

Performance Optimization

Git Garbage Collection

Git periodically runs a "garbage collection" process to optimize your repository. You can manually trigger this with:

```
git gc
```

Prune

The `git prune` command removes objects that are no longer referenced in your repository:

```
git prune
```

Compression

You can compress your repository to save disk space:

```
git gc --aggressive
```

Optimize Fetching

If you're working with a large repository, you can optimize fetching by using `--depth` to limit the history:

```
git fetch --depth=1
```

Conclusion

Git is an incredibly powerful tool with a wealth of advanced features. This chapter has covered a wide range of these features, from internal Git mechanics to integration with other tools and advanced workflows.

Remember, while these advanced techniques can be powerful, they should be used judiciously. Always consider the needs of your project and team when deciding to implement advanced Git features or workflows.

As you continue your Git journey, don't be afraid to experiment with these advanced techniques in a safe environment. The more you practice and explore, the more proficient you'll become with Git, and the more value you'll be able to derive from this powerful version control system.

In our final chapter, we'll look at some case studies and real-world scenarios where these advanced techniques have been applied, providing concrete examples of how to leverage Git's full potential in various development contexts.

Chapter 9: Git in Practice: Case Studies and Real-World Applications

Introduction

Throughout this book, we've explored Git from its basic concepts to its most advanced features. In this final chapter, we'll bring everything together by examining real-world case studies and practical applications of Git. We'll look at how different organizations and projects use Git to solve complex problems, streamline their workflows, and manage large-scale development efforts. These case studies will provide concrete examples of how to apply the concepts and techniques we've discussed in previous chapters.

Case Study 1: Managing a Large Open Source Project

Let's examine how the Linux kernel project, one of the largest and most active open source projects, uses Git to manage contributions from thousands of developers worldwide.

Background

The Linux kernel project switched to Git in 2005, when Linus Torvalds created Git specifically for Linux kernel development. The project involves:

Thousands of contributors worldwide

Frequent releases (every 2-3 months)

Multiple supported versions

A need for strict code quality control

Git Workflow

The Linux kernel project uses a hierarchical model with multiple levels of maintainers:

Developers work on patches and submit them to subsystem maintainers.

Subsystem maintainers collect, review, and test these patches, then send them up to higher-level maintainers.

Linus Torvalds, at the top of the hierarchy, pulls changes from these trusted lieutenants.

Key Git Techniques Used

Mailing List-Based Workflow: Patches are sent and discussed via mailing lists, using `git format-patch` and `git send-email`.

Signed Commits: The project requires signed commits to ensure the authenticity of contributions.

Git Describe: Used to generate descriptive version names based on the most recent tag and number of commits.

Custom Scripts: The project uses several custom scripts built around Git to manage the workflow, like `get_maintainer.pl` to identify the appropriate maintainers for a patch.

Lessons Learned

A distributed version control system like Git is crucial for managing large, globally distributed projects.

Clear contribution guidelines and a well-defined hierarchy can help manage the complexity of large projects.

Custom tooling built around Git can enhance and streamline complex workflows.

Case Study 2: Implementing GitOps in a Cloud-Native Environment

Next, let's look at how a fictional company, CloudNative Inc., implemented GitOps principles using Git as the single source of truth for their entire infrastructure.

Background

CloudNative Inc. is a medium-sized software company that decided to move to a cloud-native architecture and implement GitOps practices. Their goals were to:

Improve deployment frequency and reliability

Enhance audit trails and compliance

Simplify rollbacks and disaster recovery

Implementation

The company implemented the following strategy:

All infrastructure defined as code (using Terraform and Kubernetes manifests)

Git repositories structure:

`infra-repo`: Contains all infrastructure-as-code

`app-repos`: One for each application, containing application code and deployment manifests

CI/CD pipelines triggered by Git events

Automated sync between Git state and cluster state using a GitOps operator (Flux)

Key Git Techniques Used

Branch Protection Rules: Enforced on the `main` branch of all repositories to ensure all changes go through code review.

Git Hooks: Pre-commit hooks to run linters and validators on infrastructure code.

Git Submodules: Used in the `infra-repo` to reference specific versions of each `app-repo`.

Signed Commits: Required for all changes to production-related branches.

Git Tagging: Used to mark releases and trigger deployments.

Results

Deployment frequency increased from once a week to multiple times per day

Mean Time To Recovery (MTTR) reduced by 60% due to easy rollbacks

Audit compliance significantly improved with Git history serving as an audit trail

Lessons Learned

Git can serve as a single source of truth not just for application code, but for entire infrastructures.

Integrating Git workflows with infrastructure management requires careful planning but can yield significant benefits.

Automation and GitOps practices can significantly improve deployment frequency and reliability.

Case Study 3: Monorepo Management in a Large Enterprise

Let's examine how a large enterprise, MegaCorp, manages a monorepo containing code for hundreds of projects.

Background

MegaCorp is a multinational corporation with over 10,000 developers working on hundreds of projects. They decided to move to a monorepo structure to:

Simplify dependency management

Encourage code reuse across projects

Streamline their CI/CD processes

Challenges

The repository grew to over 1TB in size

Clone and checkout times became prohibitively long

CI/CD pipelines were taking hours to run, even for small changes

Solutions Implemented

Shallow Clones: Developers are encouraged to use shallow clones for day-to-day work:

```
git                  clone              --depth         1
https://github.com/megacorp/monorepo.git
```

Sparse Checkouts: Developers only check out the parts of the repository they need:

```
git sparse-checkout set path/to/project
```

Git LFS: Large binary files are managed using Git LFS to reduce repository size.

Custom Build System: Developed a custom build system that can determine which projects are affected by a change and only build and test those projects.

Caching: Implemented aggressive caching in CI/CD pipelines to speed up builds.

Branch Management: Implemented a trunk-based development model with short-lived feature branches to minimize merge conflicts.

Key Git Techniques Used

Partial Clone: Used to reduce initial clone times:

```
git              clone            --filter=blob:none
https://github.com/megacorp/monorepo.git
```

Git Hooks: Implemented pre-commit hooks to enforce code style and run fast, local tests.

Submodules: Some large, relatively independent projects are managed as submodules to reduce mainline repository size.

Custom Git Commands: Developed custom Git commands to simplify common operations in the monorepo.

Results

Initial clone times reduced from hours to minutes

CI/CD pipeline times reduced by 70% on average

Code reuse increased significantly across projects

Lessons Learned

Monorepos can offer significant benefits but require careful management and tooling, especially at large scales.

Git's advanced features like partial clones and sparse checkouts are crucial for managing very large repositories.

Custom tooling built around Git is often necessary to handle the unique challenges of a monorepo.

Case Study 4: Implementing Feature Flags with Git

Let's look at how a web development agency, WebWizards Inc., implemented a feature flag system integrated with their Git workflow.

Background

WebWizards Inc. builds and maintains websites for multiple clients. They wanted to implement feature flags to:

Enable easier A/B testing

Allow for gradual rollouts of new features

Facilitate trunk-based development

Implementation

Created a separate Git repository for feature flag configurations.

Developed a simple JSON-based feature flag system:

```
json
```

```json
{
  "newHeader": {
    "enabled": false,
    "users": ["beta-testers"]
  },
  "recommendationEngine": {
    "enabled": true,
    "percentage": 50
  }
}
```

Implemented a CI/CD pipeline that deploys feature flag changes immediately.

Created a custom Git hook to validate feature flag JSON before commit.

Key Git Techniques Used

Git Hooks: Pre-commit hook to validate feature flag JSON:

bash

```
#!/bin/sh

files=$(git   diff   --cached   --name-only   --diff-
filter=ACM | grep '.json$')

if [ -n "$files" ]; then

for file in $files; do

if ! jq empty "$file" >/dev/null 2>&1; then

echo "Error: Invalid JSON in $file"

exit 1

fi

done

fi
```

Git Branching: Used short-lived feature branches for developing new features, with feature flags allowing incomplete features to be merged to main.

Git Tagging: Used tags to mark different versions of the feature flag configurations, allowing easy rollback.

Results

Reduced time-to-market for new features by 40%

Increased experiment velocity, running 3x more A/B tests

Improved stability by allowing quick disabling of problematic features

Lessons Learned

Integrating feature flags with Git workflows can significantly improve development agility.

Storing feature flags in a separate repository allows for independent versioning and rollback.

Automation and validation are key to managing feature flags effectively.

Case Study 5: Git in Game Development

Let's examine how a game development studio, GameMasters Studios, uses Git to manage their complex game development process.

Background

GameMasters Studios is developing a large, open-world game with:

A team of 200+ developers

Large binary assets (textures, models, etc.)

Multiple platforms (PC, consoles, mobile)

Frequent updates and DLC releases

Challenges

Large binary files causing repository bloat

Long build times

Managing platform-specific code

Coordinating work across multiple teams (engine, gameplay, art, etc.)

Solutions Implemented

Git LFS: Used for managing large binary assets.

Branch Strategy:

`main`: Always represents shippable game

`develop`: Integration branch for features

`feature/*`: For new features

`release/*`: For preparing releases

`hotfix/*`: For critical bug fixes

`platform/*`: For platform-specific code

Submodules: Core engine maintained as a submodule.

Build System: Custom build system that uses Git metadata to determine what needs to be rebuilt.

Asset Pipeline: Custom tools to optimize assets based on target platform.

Key Git Techniques Used

Git LFS: For managing large binary files:

```
git lfs track "*.psd"

git lfs track "*.fbx"

git lfs track "*.tga"
```

Git Attributes: Used to specify different merge strategies for different file types:

```
*.cs diff=csharp

*.fbx -diff -merge

*.unity merge=unityyamlmerge
```

Git Hooks: Pre-commit hooks to enforce code style and run static analysis.

Partial Clones: To improve clone times for developers who don't need the full asset history:

```
git            clone              --filter=blob:none
https://github.com/gamemasters/awesome-game.git
```

Results

Reduced repository size by 70% after moving large assets to Git LFS

Build times reduced by 50% due to smart rebuilding based on Git metadata

Improved collaboration between different teams

Lessons Learned

Git can be effective for game development, but requires careful setup and custom tooling.

Managing large binary assets is a key challenge in game development, and Git LFS is crucial.

A well-defined branching strategy is essential for managing the complexity of game development.

Case Study 6: Git in Regulatory Compliance

Finally, let's look at how a financial services company, SecureBank, uses Git to help maintain regulatory compliance.

Background

SecureBank operates in a highly regulated industry and needs to:

Maintain detailed audit trails of all changes

Ensure separation of duties

Provide evidence of code review and approval processes

Securely manage sensitive configuration data

Implementation

Repository Structure:

Separate repositories for different applications

Configuration data in a separate, highly restricted repository

Branching Strategy:

`main`: Represents the current production state

`develop`: Integration branch

`feature/*`: For new features

`release/*`: For release candidates

Access Control: Implemented fine-grained access control using GitHub's CODEOWNERS feature.

Automation: Extensive use of CI/CD pipelines for testing, security scanning, and deployment.

Key Git Techniques Used

Signed Commits: All commits must be GPG signed:

```
git config --global commit.gpgsign true
```

Protected Branches: Strict protection rules on `main` and `release/*` branches, requiring multiple approvals and passing status checks.

Git Hooks: Server-side hooks to enforce policy compliance:

bash

```bash
#!/bin/sh

if ! grep -q "Ticket: [A-Z]+-[0-9]+" "$1"; then

echo "Commit message must reference a ticket number"

exit 1

fi
```

Git Notes: Used to attach audit information to commits:

```
git notes add -m "Reviewed by: John Doe, Jane Smith"
<commit-hash>
```

Git Cryptography: Sensitive configuration data encrypted using git-crypt.

Results

Successfully passed multiple regulatory audits

Improved traceability of all code changes

Enhanced security posture with encrypted sensitive data

Lessons Learned

Git can be a powerful tool for maintaining regulatory compliance when properly configured.

Automation and strict policies are key to ensuring consistent compliance.

Additional tools (like git-crypt) may be necessary to handle sensitive data in Git.

Conclusion

These case studies demonstrate the versatility of Git and its ability to adapt to a wide range of development scenarios.

From managing large open-source projects to ensuring regulatory compliance in financial services, Git provides the tools and flexibility to meet diverse needs.

Key takeaways from these case studies include:

Git's advanced features (LFS, submodules, hooks, etc.) are crucial for managing complex projects.

Custom tooling and automation built around Git can significantly enhance its capabilities.

Careful planning of repository structure and branching strategies is essential for successful Git usage at scale.

Git can be integrated with various tools and processes to support different development methodologies and requirements.

While Git is powerful, it often requires additional tools and practices to fully meet the needs of large or specialized projects.

As you apply Git in your own projects, remember that these case studies are not prescriptive solutions, but rather examples to learn from. Every project and organization has unique needs, and the key to success with Git is understanding its capabilities and creatively applying them to your specific situation.

With this, we conclude our journey through Git. From basic commands to advanced techniques, and now real-world applications, you have gained a comprehensive understanding of Git. Armed with this knowledge, you are well-equipped to leverage Git effectively in your own development projects, no matter their scale or complexity.

Chapter 10: The Future of Git and Version Control

Introduction

As we reach the conclusion of our comprehensive journey through Git, it's time to look back at what we've learned and cast our gaze forward to the future of Git and version control. In this final chapter, we'll recap the key concepts we've covered, discuss the current state of Git, explore emerging trends in version control, and speculate about what the future might hold for Git and similar systems.

Recap of Key Concepts

Throughout this book, we've covered a wide range of topics related to Git. Let's briefly revisit some of the key concepts:

Basic Git Operations

We started with the fundamentals: initializing repositories, making commits, understanding the staging area, and working with branches. These core concepts form the foundation of Git usage:

bash

```
git init

git add .
```

```
git commit -m "Initial commit"

git branch feature-branch

git checkout feature-branch
```

Advanced Git Features

As we progressed, we delved into more advanced features like rebasing, cherry-picking, and using interactive staging:

bash

```
git rebase main

git cherry-pick commit-hash

git add -i
```

Git Workflows

We explored various Git workflows, from simple models to more complex ones like GitFlow and trunk-based development. We learned that the choice of workflow depends on the specific needs of the project and team.

Collaboration with Remote Repositories

We covered how to work with remote repositories, including cloning, fetching, pulling, and pushing changes:

bash

```
git clone https://github.com/user/repo.git

git fetch origin

git pull origin main

git push origin feature-branch
```

Git Internals

We took a deep dive into Git's internals, understanding objects, refs, and how Git stores and manages data:

bash

```
git cat-file -p object-hash

git ls-tree HEAD

git rev-parse HEAD
```

Troubleshooting and Recovery

We learned how to troubleshoot common issues and recover from mistakes, using tools like reflog and git fsck:

bash

```
git reflog

git fsck

git reset --hard HEAD@{2}
```

Integration and CI/CD

We explored how Git integrates with other tools, particularly in CI/CD pipelines, and how it supports modern development practices like GitOps.

Real-World Applications

Finally, we examined real-world case studies demonstrating how Git is used in various scenarios, from open-source projects to game development and regulatory compliance.

The Current State of Git

As of 2024, Git has firmly established itself as the dominant version control system in the software development industry. Its distributed nature, powerful branching and merging capabilities, and extensive ecosystem of tools and integrations have made it an indispensable tool for developers worldwide.

Git's Strengths

Distributed Nature: Git's distributed architecture allows for offline work, multiple backups, and flexible workflows.

Performance: Git is fast and efficient, even with large repositories.

Branching and Merging: Git excels at creating and merging branches, facilitating parallel development.

Ecosystem: A vast array of tools, hosting platforms, and integrations enhance Git's capabilities.

Community: A large, active community contributes to Git's development and provides support.

Current Challenges

Despite its strengths, Git faces some challenges:

Learning Curve: Git can be complex for beginners, with some advanced features being difficult to master.

Large Repositories: Very large repositories or those with many binary files can still pose performance challenges.

Monorepo Management: While Git can handle monorepos, it requires careful management and often custom tooling.

Security: As development becomes more security-focused, there's an increasing need for better built-in security features in Git.

Emerging Trends in Version Control

As we look to the future, several trends are shaping the evolution of Git and version control systems:

Enhanced Support for Large Repositories

With projects growing larger and the rise of monorepos, there's a push for better handling of large repositories. Git is evolving to address this:

Partial Clones and Sparse Checkouts: These features allow developers to work with only a portion of a large repository, improving performance.

File System Monitors: Git is working on integrating with file system monitors to speed up status operations in large working trees.

Improved Handling of Binary Files

While Git LFS (Large File Storage) has helped with managing large binary files, there's still room for improvement:

Built-in Large File Support: Future versions of Git may incorporate LFS-like functionality directly into the core system.

Better Diffing for Binary Files: Improved tools for comparing and merging binary files could be on the horizon.

Enhanced Security Features

As security becomes increasingly crucial, Git is likely to incorporate more security features:

Signed Commits and Tags: While already available, these features may become more prominent and easier to use.

Enhanced Access Controls: More granular access controls at the repository and even file level.

Built-in Secrets Management: Better handling of sensitive data within Git repositories.

Artificial Intelligence and Machine Learning Integration

AI and ML are starting to intersect with version control in interesting ways:

Intelligent Merge Conflict Resolution: AI could assist in resolving merge conflicts by learning from past resolutions.

Code Quality Checks: ML models could analyze commits for potential bugs or style issues.

Predictive Analytics: AI could help predict which parts of a codebase are likely to change or cause issues.

Improved Collaboration Tools

Git hosting platforms are continually improving their collaboration features:

Enhanced Code Review Tools: More interactive and intuitive interfaces for code reviews.

Better Visualization of Repository History: Improved tools for understanding complex branch structures and commit histories.

Real-time Collaboration: Features that allow multiple developers to work on the same files simultaneously, similar to Google Docs.

GitOps and Infrastructure as Code

The GitOps approach, where Git repositories are the source of truth for infrastructure configurations, is gaining traction:

Tighter Integration with Deployment Tools: More seamless connections between Git and tools like Kubernetes and Terraform.

Automated Compliance Checks: Built-in tools to ensure infrastructure changes meet compliance requirements.

Blockchain-Inspired Features

Some concepts from blockchain technology could influence future Git development:

Immutable History: Enhanced features to ensure the integrity and immutability of commit history.

Decentralized Repositories: Exploring ways to host repositories in a more decentralized manner.

Speculative Future Developments

Looking further into the future, we can speculate about some potential developments in Git and version control:

Quantum-Safe Cryptography

As quantum computing advances, Git may need to adopt quantum-safe cryptographic algorithms to ensure the long-term security of repositories.

Virtual and Augmented Reality Interfaces

As VR and AR technologies mature, we might see new ways of visualizing and interacting with Git repositories in three-dimensional space.

```
Imagine a VR interface where you can:

Visualize branch structures as 3D trees

"Walk through" your commit history

Collaborate with team members in a virtual space
```

Natural Language Interfaces

Advanced natural language processing could allow developers to interact with Git using conversational commands:

```
Developer: "Git, show me the changes John made last
week that affected the login system."

Git: "Certainly. Here are the relevant commits from
John in the past week that modified files in the
/login directory..."
```

Automatic Code Generation and Version Control

As AI-assisted coding becomes more prevalent, Git might evolve to better handle automatically generated code:

Specialized diff and merge tools for AI-generated code

Integration with AI coding assistants for commit message generation and code review

Cross-Platform Version Control

Git could expand beyond code to become a universal version control system:

Version control for design files, integrating directly with design tools

Document version control, competing with or integrating with tools like Google Docs

Universal diff and merge tools that work across various file types

Adaptive Version Control

Git could become smarter about how it handles different projects:

Automatically suggesting optimal workflows based on project structure and team size

Dynamically adjusting its behavior (like compression algorithms or branching strategies) based on repository contents and usage patterns

Time-Travel Debugging Integration

Git could integrate more closely with debugging tools to allow developers to easily run and test code at any point in its history:

```
git debug --at "2 weeks ago"
```

This command could set up a sandboxed environment with the code as it was two weeks ago, along with a compatible development environment.

The Role of Git in Future Development Paradigms

As we look to the future, it's worth considering how Git might adapt to and influence emerging development paradigms:

Serverless and Edge Computing

As computing moves increasingly towards serverless and edge paradigms, Git might evolve to better support these models:

Specialized workflows for deploying and versioning serverless functions

Built-in tools for managing distributed edge configurations

Internet of Things (IoT)

With the proliferation of IoT devices, Git could adapt to manage code and configurations across vast networks of devices:

Lightweight Git clients for resource-constrained devices

Tools for managing and synchronizing versions across heterogeneous device networks

Quantum Computing

As quantum computing develops, Git might need to adapt in several ways:

Quantum-resistant encryption for securing repositories

New algorithms for efficiently storing and differencing quantum code

Low-Code and No-Code Platforms

As low-code and no-code platforms become more prevalent, Git might evolve to version control these kinds of projects:

Visual diffing and merging tools for graphical programming interfaces

Version control for application logic expressed in high-level, declarative formats

Challenges and Considerations for the Future of Git

As Git evolves to meet future needs, it will face several challenges:

Maintaining Simplicity

As new features are added, there's a risk of Git becoming overly complex. Maintaining a balance between power and usability will be crucial.

Backwards Compatibility

Any changes to Git's core functionality need to maintain compatibility with existing repositories and workflows.

Performance at Scale

As repositories continue to grow in size and complexity, maintaining Git's performance will be an ongoing challenge.

Security and Privacy

With increasing concerns about security and privacy, Git will need to continually evolve its security model.

Adapting to New Development Paradigms

Git will need to remain flexible enough to adapt to new ways of developing software that we haven't even imagined yet.

Conclusion: The Enduring Importance of Version Control

As we conclude our exploration of Git and look towards its future, it's clear that version control will remain a fundamental part of software development. While the specific tools and techniques may evolve, the core principles of tracking changes, managing collaboration, and maintaining a history of development will continue to be crucial.

Git has succeeded because it embodies these principles while providing the flexibility to adapt to a wide range of development workflows. Its distributed nature, powerful branching model, and extensive ecosystem have made it the de facto standard for version control.

As we move into the future, Git will likely continue to evolve, incorporating new technologies and adapting to new development paradigms. However, its core strengths – the ability to track changes, facilitate collaboration, and maintain a clear history of development – will remain as relevant as ever.

For developers, staying abreast of Git's evolution will be crucial. The skills you've learned throughout this book provide a strong foundation, but the learning journey never truly ends. As Git incorporates new features and adapts to new challenges, continuing to deepen your understanding and refine your skills will be key to making the most of this powerful tool.

Remember, Git is not just a tool, but a way of thinking about software development. It encourages clear communication, thoughtful organization of code, and a structured approach to managing changes. These principles will serve you well, regardless of how version control tools evolve in the future.

As we close this book, I encourage you to continue exploring, experimenting, and pushing the boundaries of what's possible with Git. Share your knowledge with others, contribute to the Git community, and be part of shaping the future of version control. The journey of mastering Git is ongoing, and the skills you develop will be invaluable throughout your career in software development and beyond.

Thank you for joining me on this deep dive into Git. Here's to many more commits, branches, and successful merges in your future!

Chapter 11: Git Command Reference and Cheat Sheets

Introduction

This chapter serves as a comprehensive reference for Git commands and provides several cheat sheets for quick consultation. Whether you're a beginner looking to reinforce your knowledge or an experienced user needing a quick reminder, this chapter aims to be your go-to resource for Git commands and workflows.

Git Command Reference

Setup and Configuration

Initialize a new Git repository:

```
git init
```

Configure user name:

```
git config --global user.name "Your Name"
```

Configure user email:

```
git            config            --global            user.email
"your.email@example.com"
```

Set default editor:

```
git config --global core.editor "code --wait"
```

Basic Snapshotting

Check status of working directory:

```
git status
```

Add files to staging area:

```
git add <file>
git add .  # Add all files
```

Commit changes:

```
git commit -m "Commit message"
```

Remove files:

```
git rm <file>
```

Move or rename files:

```
git mv <old-file> <new-file>
```

Branching and Merging

List branches:

```
git branch
```

Create a new branch:

```
git branch <branch-name>
```

Switch to a branch:

```
git checkout <branch-name>
```

Create and switch to a new branch:

```
git checkout -b <branch-name>
```

Merge a branch into the current branch:

```
git merge <branch-name>
```

215

Delete a branch:

```
git branch -d <branch-name>
```

Sharing and Updating Projects

Clone a repository:

```
git clone <repository-url>
```

Fetch changes from a remote:

```
git fetch <remote>
```

Pull changes from a remote:

```
git pull <remote> <branch>
```

Push changes to a remote:

```
git push <remote> <branch>
```

Add a remote:

```
git remote add <name> <url>
```

Inspection and Comparison

Show commit history:

```
git log
```

Show changes between commits, commit and working tree, etc:

```
git diff
```

Show information about any git object:

```
git show <object>
```

Patching

Create a patch:

```
git format-patch -1 <commit>
```

Apply a patch:

```
git apply <patch-file>
```

Debugging

Show who changed what and when in a file:

```
git blame <file>
```

Use binary search to find the commit that introduced a bug:

```
git bisect start

git bisect bad

git bisect good <commit>
```

Advanced Operations

Rebase commits:

```
git rebase <base>
```

Interactive rebase:

```
git rebase -i <base>
```

Cherry-pick a commit:

```
git cherry-pick <commit>
```

Create a tag:

```
git tag <tag-name>
```

Stash changes:

```
git stash
```

Apply stashed changes:

```
git stash apply
```

Git Workflow Cheat Sheets

Basic Git Workflow

Check status: `git status`

Stage changes: `git add <file>` or `git add .`

Commit changes: `git commit -m "Commit message"`

Push changes: `git push origin <branch>`

Feature Branch Workflow

Create and switch to a new branch: `git checkout -b feature-branch`

Make changes and commit: `git commit -am "Add new feature"`

Push the branch: `git push -u origin feature-branch`

Create a pull request (on GitHub/GitLab/etc.)

After review, merge the pull request

Delete the branch: `git branch -d feature-branch`

Gitflow Workflow

Start a new feature:

```
git checkout develop
git checkout -b feature/new-feature
```

Finish a feature:

```
git checkout develop
git merge feature/new-feature
```

Start a release:

```
git checkout develop
git checkout -b release/0.1.0
```

Finish a release:

```
git checkout main

git merge release/0.1.0

git checkout develop

git merge release/0.1.0

git branch -d release/0.1.0
```

Create a hotfix:

```
git checkout main

git checkout -b hotfix/bug-fix
```

Finish a hotfix:

```
git checkout main

git merge hotfix/bug-fix

git checkout develop

git merge hotfix/bug-fix

git branch -d hotfix/bug-fix
```

Forking Workflow

221

Fork the repository (on GitHub/GitLab/etc.)

Clone your fork: `git clone https://github.com/your-username/repo.git`

Add the original repo as upstream:

```
git remote add upstream https://github.com/original-owner/repo.git
```

Create a feature branch: `git checkout -b feature-branch`

Make changes and commit: `git commit -am "Add new feature"`

Push to your fork: `git push origin feature-branch`

Create a pull request to the original repo

Common Git Scenarios and Solutions

Undo last commit (keeping changes):

```
git reset HEAD~
```

Undo last commit (discarding changes):

```
git reset --hard HEAD~
```

Undo commits after a specific commit:

```
git reset <commit-hash>
```

Amend the last commit message:

```
git commit --amend
```

Undo staged changes:

```
git reset <file>
```

Discard changes in working directory:

```
git checkout -- <file>
```

Create a new branch from current HEAD:

```
git branch <new-branch>
```

Merge branch into current branch:

```
git merge <branch-name>
```

Abort a merge in progress:

223

```
git merge --abort
```

Show commit history with branch graph:

```
git log --oneline --graph --all
```

Show changes in a specific commit:

```
git show <commit-hash>
```

Temporarily store changes:

```
git stash
```

Reapply stashed changes:

```
git stash pop
```

Create a new tag:

```
git tag -a v1.0 -m "Version 1.0"
```

Push tags to remote:

```
git push origin --tags
```

Fetch changes without merging:

```
git fetch origin
```

Show remote repositories:

```
git remote -v
```

Remove a remote repository:

```
git remote remove <remote-name>
```

Rebase current branch onto another:

```
git rebase <base-branch>
```

Interactive rebase for cleaning up commits:

```
git rebase -i HEAD~3
```

Cherry-pick a commit from another branch:

```
git cherry-pick <commit-hash>
```

Show differences between two branches:

```
git diff branch1..branch2
```

Create a patch:

```
git format-patch -1 <commit-hash>
```

Apply a patch:

```
git apply /path/to/file.patch
```

Show who last modified each line of a file:

```
git blame <file>
```

Clean untracked files from working directory:

```
git clean -fd
```

Archive a Git repository:

```
git archive --format=zip HEAD > archive.zip
```

Conclusion

This comprehensive Git command reference and these cheat sheets should serve as a valuable resource as you work with Git. Remember, while these commands cover a wide range of Git operations, Git is a powerful tool with many more advanced features. As you become more comfortable with these commands, don't hesitate to explore Git's documentation for more advanced usage and options.

Keep this chapter handy as a quick reference when you need to refresh your memory on specific Git commands or workflows. Happy coding and version controlling!

Chapter 12: Git Best Practices for Professional Development

Introduction

As we conclude our comprehensive exploration of Git, it's crucial to discuss how to apply this knowledge in professional settings. This chapter will focus on Git best practices that can elevate your version control workflow, improve team collaboration, and maintain a high-quality codebase. We'll cover everything from commit hygiene to advanced team workflows, providing you with the tools to become a Git power user in professional environments.

Commit Best Practices

Write Meaningful Commit Messages

Good commit messages are crucial for maintaining a readable and useful project history.

Use the imperative mood in your commit message subject (e.g., "Add feature" not "Added feature")

Keep the subject line under 50 characters

Provide more detailed explanations in the commit body, if necessary

Reference issue numbers if your project uses an issue tracker

Example of a good commit message:

```
Implement automated email notifications

Add EmailService class to handle sending emails

Integrate   EmailService   with   UserController   for
welcome emails

Update configuration to include SMTP settings

Closes #123
```

Make Atomic Commits

Each commit should represent a single logical change. This makes it easier to understand, review, and potentially revert changes.

Group related changes into a single commit

If you find yourself using "and" in your commit message, you might need to split it into multiple commits

Commit Early and Often

Don't wait until you've written a large amount of code to commit. Smaller, frequent commits are easier to manage and understand.

Branching Strategies

Use Feature Branches

Develop new features or bug fixes in dedicated branches. This keeps the main branch stable and makes it easier to manage parallel development efforts.

bash

```
git checkout -b feature/new-login-system
```

Keep Branches Updated

Regularly update your feature branches with changes from the main branch to avoid large, painful merges later.

bash

```
git checkout feature/new-login-system
git merge main
```

Delete Branches After Merging

Keep your repository clean by deleting branches that are no longer needed.

bash

```
git branch -d feature/completed-feature
```

Code Review Practices

Use Pull/Merge Requests

Instead of directly merging branches, use pull requests (GitHub) or merge requests (GitLab). This facilitates code review and discussion before changes are merged.

Keep Pull Requests Small

Large pull requests are difficult to review effectively. Aim to keep your pull requests focused on a single feature or bug fix.

Use Code Review Checklists

Develop a checklist for code reviews to ensure consistency. This might include items like:

Does the code follow our style guide?

Are there adequate tests?

Is the documentation updated?

Collaboration Techniques

Use Rebase to Keep History Clean

When updating your feature branch with changes from the main branch, consider using rebase instead of merge to maintain a linear history.

bash

```
git checkout feature/my-feature

git rebase main
```

Squash Commits Before Merging

If your feature branch has many small commits, consider squashing them into a single, coherent commit before merging.

bash

```
git rebase -i HEAD~5   # Squash the last 5 commits
```

Use Git Hooks for Automation

Implement git hooks to automate tasks like running tests or linting code before commits or pushes.

Example pre-commit hook to run tests:

bash

```
#!/bin/sh
```

```
npm test

if [ $? -ne 0 ]; then

echo "Tests must pass before commit!"

exit 1

fi
```

Managing Large Repositories

Use Git LFS for Large Files

For repositories with large binary files, use Git Large File
Storage (LFS) to keep your repository size manageable.

bash

```
git lfs install

git lfs track "*.psd"
```

Implement Partial Clones

For very large repositories, use partial clones to reduce initial
clone times and disk usage.

bash

```
git              clone              --filter=blob:none
https://github.com/example/large-repo.git
```

Security Best Practices

Sign Your Commits

Use GPG to sign your commits, providing an extra layer of verification.

bash

```
git config --global user.signingkey <your-gpg-key-id>

git commit -S -m "Signed commit message"
```

Use .gitignore Effectively

Ensure that sensitive files, build artifacts, and environment-specific files are not tracked by Git.

Example .gitignore entries:

```
# Ignore configuration files

config.json




# Ignore build output

/build
```

```
# Ignore all .log files

*.log
```

Avoid Committing Secrets

Never commit passwords, API keys, or other secrets to your repository. Use environment variables or secure secret management tools instead.

Continuous Integration and Deployment

Integrate with CI/CD Pipelines

Use Git hooks or integrations to trigger CI/CD pipelines on commits or pull requests.

Example GitHub Actions workflow:

yaml

```
name: CI


on: [push, pull_request]


jobs:
```

```
build:

runs-on: ubuntu-latest

steps:

uses: actions/checkout@v2

name: Run tests

run: npm test
```

Use Tags for Releases

Use Git tags to mark release points in your code. This makes it easy to deploy specific versions.

bash

```bash
git tag -a v1.0.0 -m "Release version 1.0.0"

git push origin v1.0.0
```

Documentation Practices

Maintain a Detailed README

Keep your README file up-to-date with project setup instructions, contribution guidelines, and other relevant information.

Use GitHub/GitLab Wiki

For more extensive documentation, utilize the wiki feature provided by platforms like GitHub or GitLab.

Document Git Workflow

Create a CONTRIBUTING.md file that outlines your team's Git workflow, branching strategy, and code review process.

Advanced Git Techniques for Professional Use

Git Bisect for Debugging

Use git bisect to efficiently find the commit that introduced a bug.

bash

```bash
git bisect start

git bisect bad  # Current version is bad

git bisect good v1.0  # v1.0 is known to be good
```

Reflog for Recovery

Use git reflog to recover lost commits or branches.

bash

```bash
git reflog
```

```
git checkout -b recovered-branch <lost-commit-hash>
```

Interactive Rebase for History Cleanup

Use interactive rebase to clean up your commit history before merging a feature branch.

bash

```
git rebase -i main
```

Optimizing Git Performance

Regular Maintenance

Perform regular Git maintenance to keep your repository performant.

bash

```
git gc
git prune
```

Use Shallow Clones for CI/CD

In CI/CD environments where you don't need the full history, use shallow clones to speed up the process.

bash

```
git          clone          --depth          1
https://github.com/example/repo.git
```

Team Workflow Strategies

Gitflow for Structured Releases

Consider using Gitflow for projects with structured release cycles.

`main` branch for production-ready code

`develop` branch for ongoing development

Feature branches branched off and merged back into `develop`

Release branches for preparing releases

Hotfix branches for critical bug fixes

Trunk-Based Development for Continuous Deployment

For teams practicing continuous deployment, consider a trunk-based development approach.

Work in small batches

Merge to the main branch frequently (at least daily)

Use feature flags to manage partially-completed work

Handling Legacy Code

Create Baseline for Legacy Projects

When starting version control for a legacy project, create a baseline commit.

bash

```
git add .

git commit -m "Baseline commit of legacy code"
```

Use Git Blame Wisely

When dealing with legacy code, use `git blame` to understand the context of changes, but avoid using it to assign personal blame.

bash

```
git blame path/to/file
```

Conclusion

Mastering these Git best practices will significantly enhance your efficiency and effectiveness as a professional developer. Remember, the key to successful Git usage in a professional environment is consistency and clear communication within your team.

As you apply these practices, keep in mind that every team and project is unique. Be prepared to adapt these guidelines to fit your specific needs. Regular review and refinement of your Git processes with your team will help ensure that you're using Git to its full potential.

By following these best practices, you'll not only improve your own workflow but also contribute to a more productive and harmonious development environment for your entire team. Happy coding, and may your commits always be clean, your merges conflict-free, and your repositories well-organized!

Chapter 13: Advanced Git Scenarios and Problem-Solving

Introduction

As you progress in your Git journey, you'll inevitably encounter complex scenarios that require advanced problem-solving skills. This chapter is designed to prepare you for these situations, providing in-depth coverage of advanced Git concepts, troubleshooting techniques, and real-world problem-solving strategies. We'll explore scenarios that experienced developers often face and provide detailed solutions to help you navigate these challenges confidently.

Advanced Rebase Scenarios

Rebasing is a powerful Git feature, but it can lead to complex situations. Let's explore some advanced rebase scenarios and how to handle them.

Interactive Rebasing for History Cleanup

Scenario: You've made several commits on a feature branch, but the commit history is messy and contains unnecessary commits.

Solution: Use interactive rebasing to clean up your commit history before merging.

bash

```
git checkout feature-branch
git rebase -i main
```

This will open an editor with a list of commits. You can then:

Reorder commits by changing their order in the file

Squash commits by changing 'pick' to 'squash' or 's'

Edit commit messages by changing 'pick' to 'reword' or 'r'

Delete commits by removing the line

Example:

```
pick 2c3a951 Add initial implementation of feature X
squash 3d4b862 Fix typo in feature X
squash 5e6c973 Refactor feature X
pick 7f8d084 Implement feature Y
reword 9g0h195 Add tests for feature X and Y
```

After saving and closing the editor, Git will apply these changes, potentially opening new editor windows for you to modify commit messages.

Best Practice: Always perform interactive rebases on branches that haven't been pushed to a shared repository, or communicate clearly with your team if you need to rebase a shared branch.

Resolving Complex Conflicts During Rebase

Scenario: You're rebasing a long-running feature branch onto the latest main, and you encounter multiple complex merge conflicts.

Solution: Resolve conflicts step-by-step, using Git's conflict resolution tools and your understanding of the codebase.

Start the rebase:

bash

```
git rebase main
```

When you encounter a conflict, Git will pause the rebase. Use `git status` to see which files are conflicting.

Open the conflicting files and look for conflict markers (`<<<<<<<`, `=======`, `>>>>>>>`). Resolve the conflicts manually, keeping the correct code and removing the conflict markers.

244

After resolving conflicts in a file, stage it:

bash

```
git add resolved-file.js
```

Continue the rebase:

bash

```
git rebase --continue
```

Repeat steps 3-5 for each conflict until the rebase is complete.

If at any point you make a mistake or feel overwhelmed:

Use `git rebase --abort` to cancel the rebase and return to the pre-rebase state.

Use `git reflog` to find the commit hash from before the rebase started, and reset to it:

bash

```
git reset --hard <pre-rebase-commit-hash>
```

Best Practice: Before starting a complex rebase, create a backup branch:

245

```bash
```

```bash
git branch backup-feature-branch feature-branch
```

This allows you to easily recover if the rebase goes wrong.

Advanced Merging Techniques

Merging is a fundamental Git operation, but there are advanced techniques that can help in complex scenarios.

Octopus Merge

Scenario: You need to merge changes from multiple feature branches simultaneously.

Solution: Use an octopus merge, which allows you to merge more than two branches at once.

```bash
```

```bash
git checkout main

git merge feature1 feature2 feature3
```

This creates a merge commit with multiple parents. It's useful when you need to integrate several independent changes at once.

Note: Octopus merges can't handle merge conflicts. If conflicts occur, you'll need to merge the branches one by one.

Subtree Merging

Scenario: You want to merge a project into your main project as a subdirectory, while keeping the commit histories separate.

Solution: Use subtree merging.

Add the other project as a remote:

bash

```
git remote add other-project
https://github.com/user/other-project.git
```

Fetch the other project:

bash

```
git fetch other-project
```

Merge the other project into a subdirectory:

bash

```
git merge -s subtree --squash --allow-unrelated-
histories other-project/main
```

Commit the merge:

bash

```
git commit -m "Merge other-project as a subdirectory"
```

This brings in the current state of the other project without its commit history. You can then push changes back to the other project using subtree commands.

Git Internals and Low-Level Operations

Understanding Git's internals can help you solve complex problems and recover from seemingly catastrophic situations.

Recovering Lost Commits

Scenario: You've accidentally reset your branch to an earlier commit, losing several important commits in the process.

Solution: Use Git's reflog and low-level commands to recover the lost commits.

Check the reflog to find the lost commits:

bash

```
git reflog
```

Once you've identified the hash of the commit you want to recover, you can create a new branch pointing to that commit:

bash

```
git branch recovered-branch <commit-hash>
```

Alternatively, you can reset your current branch to that commit:

bash

```
git reset --hard <commit-hash>
```

Remember, the reflog only keeps entries for a limited time (usually 30 days for unreachable commits), so act quickly if you need to recover lost work.

Repairing Corrupted Git Repositories

Scenario: Your Git repository has become corrupted, and basic Git commands are failing.

Solution: Use Git's fsck (file system check) and low-level plumbing commands to identify and repair the issues.

Run a file system check:

bash

```
git fsck --full
```

This will report any corrupt objects.

If you find corrupt objects, you may be able to recover them from a remote repository:

bash

```
git fetch origin
```

If that doesn't work, you might need to manually remove the corrupt objects. Be very careful with this step, as it can lead to data loss:

bash

```
rm
.git/objects/XX/YYYYYYYYYYYYYYYYYYYYYYYYYYYYYYYYYYYYYY
YYYY
```

Replace XX with the first two characters of the corrupt object's hash, and YYYYYY... with the rest.

After removing corrupt objects, try repacking the repository:

bash

```
git repack -a -d
```

If all else fails, you may need to clone a fresh of the repository and manually over your recent (uncommitted) changes.

Best Practice: Regularly push your changes to a remote repository to have a backup in case of local repository corruption.

Advanced Branch Management

Managing branches in large projects or complex workflows can be challenging. Here are some advanced techniques to help.

Managing Long-Running Feature Branches

Scenario: You're working on a long-running feature branch that's fallen far behind the main branch.

Solution: Regularly integrate changes from the main branch to avoid a painful merge later.

Fetch the latest changes from the remote:

bash

```
git fetch origin
```

Rebase your feature branch onto the latest main:

bash

```
git checkout feature-branch

git rebase origin/main
```

If you encounter conflicts, resolve them as described in the rebase section earlier.

Force-push your rebased branch (be careful with this on shared branches):

bash

```
git push --force-with-lease origin feature-branch
```

Best Practice: Communicate with your team before force-pushing to a shared branch, and consider creating a new branch instead of force-pushing if others are actively working on the same branch.

Creating and Managing Release Branches

Scenario: You need to create a release branch for an upcoming version, while continuing development on the main branch.

Solution: Use a release branching strategy.

Create a release branch from the main branch:

bash

```
git checkout -b release-1.0 main
```

Make any necessary last-minute changes or version bumps on this branch.

When ready to release, merge the release branch into main and create a tag:

bash

```
git checkout main

git merge release-1.0

git tag -a v1.0 -m "Release version 1.0"
```

Also merge the release branch back into the development branch (if you're using one):

bash

```
git checkout develop

git merge release-1.0
```

Delete the release branch when it's no longer needed:

bash

```
git branch -d release-1.0
```

This strategy allows you to freeze the code for a release while continuing development for the next release on the main or development branch.

Git Workflows for Large Teams

As team size grows, coordinating work becomes more challenging. Here are some advanced workflow strategies for large teams.

Implementing a Gitflow Workflow

Scenario: Your large team needs a structured workflow to manage features, releases, and hotfixes.

Solution: Implement the Gitflow workflow, which defines specific branch roles and interactions.

Set up the workflow:

bash

```
git flow init
```

This will prompt you to specify branch names for production, development, features, releases, and hotfixes.

Start a new feature:

bash

```
git flow feature start new-feature
```

Finish a feature:

bash

```
git flow feature finish new-feature
```

Start a release:

bash

```
git flow release start 1.0
```

Finish a release:

bash

```
git flow release finish 1.0
```

Create a hotfix:

bash

```
git flow hotfix start bug-fix
```

Finish a hotfix:

bash

```
git flow hotfix finish bug-fix
```

Gitflow provides a structured approach to branching and merging, which can be particularly helpful for teams with scheduled releases.

Trunk-Based Development for Continuous Deployment

Scenario: Your team wants to implement continuous deployment and needs a Git workflow to support it.

Solution: Adopt a trunk-based development approach.

All developers work on short-lived feature branches (or directly on the main branch for very small changes).

Continuously integrate changes into the main branch:

bash

```
git checkout main

git pull origin main

git merge feature-branch

git push origin main
```

Use feature flags in your code to hide incomplete features in production.

Set up automated tests and deployment pipelines triggered by pushes to the main branch.

This approach supports rapid iteration and deployment, but requires disciplined developers and robust automated testing.

Git in Specialized Environments

Git can be adapted to various specialized development environments. Here are some advanced scenarios you might encounter.

Git for Data Science and Machine Learning

Scenario: You're working on a data science project with large datasets and model files.

Solution: Use Git in combination with Git LFS and DVC (Data Version Control).

Set up Git LFS for large files:

bash

```
git lfs install
git lfs track "*.csv" "*.pkl" "*.h5"
```

Use DVC for data and model versioning:

bash

```
dvc init

dvc add data/large_dataset.csv

dvc add models/trained_model.pkl
```

Commit both Git and DVC changes:

bash

```
git add .
git commit -m "Add dataset and trained model"
```

Push to both Git and DVC remotes:

bash

```
git push origin main
dvc push
```

This setup allows you to version control your code with Git, your large files with Git LFS, and your data and models with DVC.

Git for Game Development

Scenario: You're working on a game with large binary assets and need to manage multiple versions for different platforms.

Solution: Use Git with LFS and a branching strategy for different platforms.

Set up Git LFS for large game assets:

bash

```
git lfs install

git lfs track "*.fbx" "*.png" "*.wav"
```

Create branches for different platforms:

bash

```
git branch pc-version

git branch mobile-version

git branch console-version
```

Use sparse checkout to work with platform-specific assets:

bash

```
git config core.sparsecheckout true

echo "common/*" >> .git/info/sparse-checkout

echo "pc/*" >> .git/info/sparse-checkout
```

```
git read-tree -mu HEAD
```

When making cross-platform changes, use cherry-picking to apply changes to other platform branches:

bash

```
git cherry-pick <commit-hash>
```

This setup allows you to manage large game assets efficiently and maintain separate but related codebases for different platforms.

Git in Regulated Environments

In regulated industries like finance or healthcare, you may need to adapt your Git workflow to meet compliance requirements.

Implementing a Compliant Git Workflow

Scenario: You need to implement a Git workflow that meets regulatory requirements for change management and auditing.

Solution: Implement a strictly controlled workflow with signed commits, protected branches, and comprehensive logging.

Require signed commits:

bash

```
git config --global commit.gpgsign true
```

Set up protected branches in your Git hosting platform (e.g., GitHub, GitLab) to require:

Signed commits

Multiple approvals for pull requests

Passing status checks before merging

Implement server-side hooks to enforce policy, e.g., requiring ticket numbers in commit messages:

bash

```
#!/bin/sh

commit_msg=$(cat $1)

if ! echo "$commit_msg" | grep -qE "TICKET-[0-9]+";
then

echo "Commit message must include a ticket number
(e.g., TICKET-123)"

exit 1

fi
```

Set up comprehensive logging and auditing:

Use Git notes to attach audit information to commits:

bash

```
git notes add -m "Reviewed by: John Doe" <commit-hash>
```

Implement a post-receive hook to log all pushes to a secure, tamper-evident storage system.

Regularly back up your entire Git repository, including all refs and reflogs.

This setup provides a high level of control and auditability, suitable for regulated environments.

Recovering from Git Disasters

Even with best practices in place, disasters can happen. Here's how to recover from some worst-case scenarios.

Recovering from an Accidental Force Push

Scenario: Someone has force-pushed to a shared branch, overwriting important commits.

Solution: Use the reflog to recover the lost commits and carefully restore the branch.

Identify the lost commits using the reflog:

bash

```
git reflog show origin/main
```

Create a new branch at the commit before the force push:

bash

```
git branch recovery-branch <commit-hash>
```

Cherry-pick the lost commits onto this new branch:

bash

```
git cherry-pick <lost-commit-hash>
```

Once you've recovered all lost commits, merge the recovery branch into the main branch:

bash

```
git checkout main
git merge recovery-branch
```

Force-push the corrected history (communicate with your team first):

bash

```
git push --force-with-lease origin main
```

Chapter 14: Git in Enterprise Environments and Large-Scale Projects

Introduction

As organizations grow and projects scale, the complexity of version control increases exponentially. This chapter delves into the intricacies of using Git in enterprise environments and large-scale projects. We'll explore advanced techniques, best practices, and strategies for managing Git across large teams, multiple projects, and complex organizational structures. Whether you're a DevOps engineer, a team lead, or an enterprise architect, this chapter will provide you with the knowledge to leverage Git effectively in even the most demanding environments.

Enterprise-Grade Git Infrastructure

Selecting and Setting Up Git Servers

In enterprise environments, choosing the right Git server is crucial. Options include:

GitHub Enterprise: Offers features like LDAP integration, audit logging, and SAML single sign-on.

GitLab Enterprise Edition: Provides CI/CD pipelines, container registry, and advanced security features.

Bitbucket Server: Integrates well with other Atlassian products and offers fine-grained permissions.

Self-hosted solutions: Like Gitea or Gogs, which can be customized to fit specific enterprise needs.

When setting up your Git server:

Ensure high availability and load balancing:

bash

```
# Example: Setting up HAProxy for load balancing Git
servers

frontend git_frontend

bind *:80

mode tcp

default_backend git_backend


backend git_backend

mode tcp

balance roundrobin

server git1 192.168.1.1:22 check

server git2 192.168.1.2:22 check
```

Implement robust backup and disaster recovery procedures:

bash

```
# Example: Automated daily backups

0 2 * * * /usr/local/bin/gitlab-backup create CRON=1
```

Set up monitoring and alerting:

bash

```
# Example: Prometheus configuration for monitoring
Git server

job_name: 'gitlab'

static_configs:

targets: ['gitlab.example.com:9090']
```

Scalable Authentication and Authorization

Implement scalable authentication and authorization:

Integrate with enterprise identity providers:

yaml

```
# Example: LDAP configuration in GitLab
```

```ruby
gitlab_rails['ldap_enabled'] = true

gitlab_rails['ldap_servers'] = {

'main' => {

'label' => 'LDAP',

'host' =>  'ldap.example.com',

'port' => 389,

'uid' => 'sAMAccountName',

'bind_dn'                    =>                'CN=Service
Account,OU=Users,DC=example,DC=com',

'password' => 'password',

'encryption' => 'simple_tls',

'base' => 'OU=Users,DC=example,DC=com'

}

}
```

Implement Single Sign-On (SSO):

ruby

```ruby
# Example: SAML configuration in GitHub Enterprise

github_enterprise['saml'] = {

'sso_url' => 'https://idp.example.com/saml/sso',
```

```
'certificate'                                      =>
'MIICYDCCAgigAwIBAgIBADANBgkqhkiG9w0...',

'issuer' => 'https://github.example.com',

'name_identifier_format'                           =>
'urn:oasis:names:tc:SAML:1.1:nameid-
format:emailAddress'

}
```

Set up fine-grained access controls:

sql

```sql
Example: Creating a custom role in Bitbucket Server

INSERT INTO sta_normal_group (id, name, description)

VALUES (50, 'Developers', 'Read and write access to
all repositories');


INSERT INTO sta_permission (id, name, description)

VALUES (60, 'REPO_READ', 'Read access to
repositories');


INSERT INTO sta_normal_group_permission (group_id,
permission_id)

VALUES (50, 60);
```

High-Performance Git Storage

Optimize Git storage for large-scale repositories:

Implement Git object storage on high-performance SSD arrays:

bash

```
# Example: Moving Git object storage to a dedicated
SSD volume

mv  /var/opt/gitlab/git-data/repositories  /mnt/git-
ssd/repositories

ln -s /mnt/git-ssd/repositories /var/opt/gitlab/git-
data/repositories
```

Use Git alternates for shared objects across multiple repositories:

bash

```
# Example: Setting up Git alternates

echo              /path/to/shared/objects              >
/path/to/repo/.git/objects/info/alternates
```

Implement regular Git garbage collection and repack operations:

bash

```
# Example: Scheduled Git maintenance

0 3 * * * find /path/to/repos -name "*.git" -type d -
exec git --git-dir={} gc --aggressive \;
```

Advanced Git Workflows for Large Teams

Implementing GitFlow at Scale

Adapt GitFlow for large-scale projects:

Set up branch protection rules:

yaml

```
# Example: Branch protection rule in GitHub

branches:

name: main

protection:

required_pull_request_reviews:

required_approving_review_count: 2

required_status_checks:

strict: true

contexts: ["ci/jenkins", "security/snyk"]
```

```
enforce_admins: true
```

Automate release branch creation:

```
python
```

```
# Example: Python script to create a release branch

import subprocess


def create_release_branch(version):
subprocess.run(["git", "checkout", "develop"])
subprocess.run(["git", "pull"])
subprocess.run(["git", "checkout", "-b", f"release-{version}"])
subprocess.run(["git", "push", "-u", "origin", f"release-{version}"])


create_release_branch("1.2.0")
```

Implement automated merging of hotfixes:

```
bash
```

```
# Example: Git hook to automatically merge hotfixes to develop
```

```sh
#!/bin/sh

# .git/hooks/post-merge

current_branch=$(git rev-parse --abbrev-ref HEAD)

if [[ $current_branch == hotfix-* ]]; then

git checkout develop

git merge $current_branch

git push origin develop

fi
```

Trunk-Based Development for Continuous Deployment

Implement trunk-based development for large teams:

Set up feature flags for incomplete features:

python

```python
# Example: Feature flag implementation

def is_feature_enabled(feature_name, user):

return FeatureFlag.objects.filter(name=feature_name, enabled=True).exists() and \

user.has_feature_access(feature_name)
```

273

```python
if is_feature_enabled('new_ui', current_user):

# New UI code

else:

# Old UI code
```

Implement comprehensive automated testing:

yaml

```yaml
# Example: GitLab CI configuration for thorough
testing

stages:

test

integration

performance


unit_tests:

stage: test

script: python -m unittest discover tests/unit


integration_tests:

stage: integration
```

```
script: python -m unittest discover tests/integration


performance_tests:

stage: performance

script: locust -f performance_tests.py --headless -u
100 -r 10 -t 5m
```

Set up automated code review tools:

yaml

```
# Example: SonarQube integration in Jenkins pipeline

pipeline {

agent any

stages {

stage('SonarQube Analysis') {

steps {

script {

def scannerHome = tool 'SonarScanner'

withSonarQubeEnv('SonarQube') {

sh "${scannerHome}/bin/sonar-scanner"

}
```

```
}

}

}

}

}
```

Managing Long-Running Feature Branches

For features that can't be completed quickly:

Implement regular rebasing:

bash

```bash
# Example: Script to rebase long-running branches

#!/bin/bash

branches=$(git branch --list 'feature/*' --format='%(refname:short)')

for branch in $branches; do

git checkout $branch

git rebase main

git push --force-with-lease origin $branch

done
```

Set up automated conflict detection:

yaml

```yaml
# Example: GitHub Action to detect conflicts

name: Detect Merge Conflicts

on:

push:

branches:

'feature/**'

jobs:

detect_conflicts:

runs-on: ubuntu-latest

steps:

uses: actions/checkout@v2

name: Check for conflicts

run: |

git fetch origin main:main

git merge-base --is-ancestor main HEAD ||

(git merge-tree $(git merge-base main HEAD) main HEAD
| grep -i "<<<<<<<" && exit 1 || exit 0)
```

Implement feature branch lifecycle policies:

python

```python
# Example: Script to notify about old feature branches

import subprocess

from datetime import datetime, timedelta


def get_old_branches():

output = subprocess.check_output(["git", "branch", "-
r",      "--list",      "origin/feature/*",      "--
format=%(refname:short) %(committerdate:iso)"])

old_branches = []

for line in output.decode().split('\n'):

if line:

branch, date_str = line.rsplit(' ', 1)

date = datetime.fromisoformat(date_str)

if datetime.now() - date > timedelta(days=30):

old_branches.append(branch)

return old_branches


old_branches = get_old_branches()

if old_branches:
```

```
print("The following branches are more than 30 days
old:")

for branch in old_branches:

print(branch)
```

Managing Monorepos in Git

Setting Up a Monorepo Structure

Organize a monorepo effectively:

Create a clear directory structure:

```
monorepo/

├── projects/

│   ├── project-a/

│   ├── project-b/

│   └── project-c/

├── shared/

│   ├── libraries/

│   └── tools/

└── docs/
```

Implement custom Git commands for monorepo
management:

bash

```bash
# Example: Custom Git command to create a new project
#!/bin/bash

# git-new-project

project_name=$1

mkdir -p projects/$project_name

touch projects/$project_name/.gitkeep

git add projects/$project_name

git commit -m "Create new project: $project_name"
```

Set up project-specific Git hooks:

bash

```bash
# Example: Pre-commit hook for a specific project
#!/bin/bash

# .git/hooks/pre-commit

if git diff --cached --name-only | grep -q
"^projects/project-a/"; then

cd projects/project-a

npm run lint
```

Optimizing Git Performance in Monorepos

Manage large monorepos efficiently:

Implement sparse-checkout for developers working on specific projects:

bash

```
# Example: Setting up sparse-checkout for a specific
project

git    clone    --filter=blob:none    --no-checkout
https://github.com/company/monorepo.git

cd monorepo

git sparse-checkout init --cone

git sparse-checkout set projects/project-a shared

git checkout main
```

Use Git's partial clone feature:

bash

```
# Example: Partial clone of a monorepo

git            clone            --filter=blob:none
https://github.com/company/monorepo.git
```

Implement Git Virtual File System (VFS) for extremely large repositories:

powershell

```
# Example: Setting up Git VFS (on Windows)

gvfs clone https://github.com/company/monorepo.git
C:\src\monorepo

cd C:\src\monorepo

git checkout main
```

Implementing CI/CD for Monorepos

Set up efficient CI/CD pipelines for monorepos:

Use build tools that support monorepo structures, like Bazel or Buck:

python

```
# Example: Bazel BUILD file for a monorepo project

load("@rules_python//python:defs.bzl", "py_binary")


py_binary(

name = "project_a_main",
```

```
srcs = ["projects/project_a/main.py"],

deps = [

"//shared/libraries:common_lib",

],

)
```

Implement intelligent build triggering:

yaml

```
# Example: GitLab CI configuration for selective
builds

.build_template: &build_template

script:

bazel build //...


project_a:

<<: *build_template

only:

changes:

projects/project_a/**/*

shared/**/*
```

```
project_b:

<<: *build_template

only:

changes:

projects/project_b/**/*

shared/**/*
```

Set up parallel testing across multiple projects:

yaml

```
# Example: Jenkins pipeline for parallel testing in a
monorepo

pipeline {

agent any

stages {

stage('Test') {

parallel {

stage('Project A') {

when { changeset "projects/project-a/**/*" }

steps {
```

```
dir('projects/project-a') {

sh 'npm test'

}

}

}

stage('Project B') {

when { changeset "projects/project-b/**/*" }

steps {

dir('projects/project-b') {

sh 'gradle test'

}

}

}

}

}

}
```

Git for Microservices Architecture

Repository Structure for Microservices

Choose between multi-repo and monorepo approaches:

Multi-repo structure:

```
company-services/
├── user-service/
├── payment-service/
├── inventory-service/
└── api-gateway/
```

Monorepo structure for microservices:

```
microservices-monorepo/
├── services/
│   ├── user-service/
│   ├── payment-service/
│   ├── inventory-service/
│   └── api-gateway/
├── shared/
│   ├── proto/
│   └── libraries/
```

```
└── deployment/
├── kubernetes/
└── terraform/
```

287

Chapter 15: Advanced Git Techniques and Integrations

Introduction

As we reach the pinnacle of our Git journey, this chapter delves into the most advanced Git techniques and integrations. We'll explore cutting-edge practices, complex scenarios, and how Git integrates with various tools and workflows in modern software development. Whether you're a seasoned Git expert looking to push the boundaries of what's possible or an aspiring power user aiming to master the intricacies of Git, this chapter will provide you with the knowledge and techniques to tackle even the most challenging version control scenarios.

Advanced Git Internals

Deep Dive into Git Objects

Git's object model is the foundation of its power. Let's explore it in depth:

Blobs: Store file content

```bash
```

```
# Create a blob object

echo "Hello, Git!" | git hash-object -w --stdin

# Output: a8a940627d132695a9769df4f5c5c573cd9c33ca


# Retrieve blob content

git                    cat-file                    -p
a8a940627d132695a9769df4f5c5c573cd9c33ca

# Output: Hello, Git!
```

Trees: Represent directories

bash

```
# Create a tree object

git    update-index    --add    --cacheinfo    100644
a8a940627d132695a9769df4f5c5c573cd9c33ca hello.txt

git write-tree

# Output: 9c435a86e664be00db0d973e981425e4a3ef3f8d


# Examine tree content

git                    cat-file                    -p
9c435a86e664be00db0d973e981425e4a3ef3f8d

#          Output:          100644          blob
a8a940627d132695a9769df4f5c5c573cd9c33ca    hello.txt
```

Commits: Point to trees and form history

bash

```
# Create a commit object

echo    "Initial    commit"    |    git    commit-tree
9c435a86e664be00db0d973e981425e4a3ef3f8d

# Output: 8d7f63d9e9ab3a67b9768103d6ba5c92a6895120


# Examine commit content

git                      cat-file                      -p
8d7f63d9e9ab3a67b9768103d6ba5c92a6895120

# Output:

# tree 9c435a86e664be00db0d973e981425e4a3ef3f8d

#    author    Your    Name    <your.email@example.com>
1631234567 +0000

#    committer    Your    Name    <your.email@example.com>
1631234567 +0000

#

# Initial commit
```

Custom Git Plumbing Commands

Create custom Git commands using plumbing commands:

Find the root commit of a branch:

bash

```bash
#!/bin/bash

# git-root-commit

branch=${1:-HEAD}
root=$(git rev-list --max-parents=0 $branch)
echo "Root commit of $branch: $root"
git show --no-patch --format="%h %s" $root
```

List all blobs larger than a specified size:

bash

```bash
#!/bin/bash

# git-large-blobs

size_limit=${1:-1M}
git rev-list --objects --all |
git cat-file --batch-check='%(objecttype) %(objectname) %(objectsize) %(rest)' |
```

```
awk -v limit=$(numfmt --from=iec $size_limit) '$3 >
limit' |

sort -k3nr |

numfmt --to=iec --field=3 |

column -t -s ' ' -o ' | '
```

Customizing Git's Internal Behavior

Modify Git's internal behavior using configuration options:

Change the hash algorithm:

bash

```
git config --global core.repositoryFormatVersion 1

git config --global extensions.objectFormat sha256
```

Customize how Git handles line endings:

bash

```
# On Windows

git config --global core.autocrlf true



# On macOS and Linux

git config --global core.autocrlf input
```

Set up custom diff drivers:

ini

```ini
# In .gitattributes

*.png diff=exif


# In .git/config or global Git config

[diff "exif"]

textconv = exiftool
```

Advanced Branching and Merging Techniques

Complex Merge Strategies

Explore advanced merge strategies for challenging scenarios:

Octopus Merge: Merging multiple branches simultaneously

bash

```bash
git merge branch1 branch2 branch3 branch4
```

Ours Merge Strategy: Keep our version in case of conflicts

bash

```
git merge -s ours obsolete-branch
```

Subtree Merge: Merge a project as a subdirectory

bash

```
git remote add sub-project https://github.com/example/sub-project.git

git fetch sub-project

git merge -s subtree --squash sub-project/main
```

Advanced Rebasing Techniques

Master complex rebasing scenarios:

Interactive Rebase with Exec: Run tests for each commit during rebase

bash

```
git rebase -i main --exec "npm test"
```

Rebase with Autosquash: Automatically squash fixup commits

bash

```bash
# Make a change and commit it as a fixup

git commit --fixup <commit-hash>



# Perform the rebase

git rebase -i --autosquash <base-branch>
```

Rebase onto an Unrelated Branch: Move a series of commits to a new base

bash

```bash
git rebase --onto new-base old-base feature-branch
```

Branch Management at Scale

Implement strategies for managing branches in large projects:

Automated branch cleanup:

bash

```bash
#!/bin/bash

# Delete local branches that have been merged into main
```

295

```
git branch --merged main | grep -v "^\*" | xargs -n 1
git branch -d


# Delete remote branches that have been merged into
main

git branch -r --merged main | grep -v main | sed
's/origin\///' | xargs -n 1 git push --delete origin
```

Branch naming conventions enforced by hooks:

bash

```bash
#!/bin/bash

# .git/hooks/pre-push


branch_name=$(git rev-parse --abbrev-ref HEAD)

valid_branch_regex="^(feature|bugfix|hotfix)\/[a-z0-
9-]+$"


if [[ ! $branch_name =~ $valid_branch_regex ]]; then

echo "Error: Branch name '$branch_name' doesn't match
the required format."

exit 1

fi
```

Automated branch synchronization:

python

```python
# sync_branches.py
import subprocess

def sync_branch(branch):
    subprocess.run(['git', 'checkout', branch])
    subprocess.run(['git', 'pull', 'origin', branch])
    subprocess.run(['git', 'merge', 'main', '--no-edit'])
    subprocess.run(['git', 'push', 'origin', branch])

branches = ['develop', 'staging', 'qa']
for branch in branches:
    sync_branch(branch)
```

Git for Specialized Workflows

Git for Data Science and Machine Learning

Adapt Git for data science and ML workflows:

Use Git LFS for large data files and models:

bash

```bash
git lfs install

git lfs track "*.csv" "*.h5" "*.pkl"

git add .gitattributes
```

Integrate with DVC (Data Version Control):

bash

```bash
dvc init

dvc add data/large_dataset.csv

git add data/.gitignore data/large_dataset.csv.dvc

git commit -m "Add dataset using DVC"
```

Version control Jupyter notebooks:

bash

```bash
# Install nbdime

pip install nbdime


# Configure Git to use nbdime for notebook diffing

nbdime config-git --enable --global
```

Git for Game Development

Adapt Git for game development workflows:

Use Git LFS for binary assets:

bash

```
git lfs install

git    lfs    track    "*.png"    "*.fbx"    "*.unity"
"*.unitypackage"

git add .gitattributes
```

Implement unity-specific .gitignore:

gitignore

```
# Unity generated

[Ll]ibrary/

[Tt]emp/

[Oo]bj/

[Bb]uild/

[Bb]uilds/

[Ll]ogs/
```

```
# Never ignore Asset meta data

![Aa]ssets/**/*.meta



# Uncomment this line if you wish to ignore the asset
store tools plugin

# [Aa]ssets/AssetStoreTools*
```

Set up Git hooks for Unity project validation:

bash

```bash
#!/bin/bash

# .git/hooks/pre-commit



# Check for Unity meta files

changes=$(git  diff  --cached  --name-only  --diff-
filter=ACM)

for file in $changes; do

if [[ $file == Assets/* && ! -f "${file}.meta" ]];
then

echo "Error: Meta file missing for $file"

exit 1

fi
```

Git for Regulatory Compliance

Implement Git workflows that meet regulatory requirements:

Enforce signed commits:

bash

```
git config --global commit.gpgsign true
```

Implement a commit message policy:

bash

```bash
#!/bin/bash

# .git/hooks/commit-msg


commit_msg=$(cat $1)

required_pattern="^(feat|fix|docs|style|refactor|test|chore)\: .+"


if ! [[ $commit_msg =~ $required_pattern ]]; then

echo "Error: Commit message format is incorrect. It should start with type: message"
```

```
exit 1

fi
```

Set up an audit trail using Git notes:

bash

```bash
#!/bin/bash

# post-commit hook to add audit information


commit_hash=$(git rev-parse HEAD)

author=$(git log -1 --format="%an <%ae>")

date=$(git log -1 --format="%ad")


git notes add -m "Audit: Committed by $author on
$date" $commit_hash
```

Advanced Git Integrations

Git with CI/CD Pipelines

Integrate Git deeply with CI/CD workflows:

GitHub Actions for advanced Git operations:

yaml

302

```yaml
name: Advanced Git CI


on: [push]


jobs:

git-operations:

runs-on: ubuntu-latest

steps:

uses: actions/checkout@v2

with:

fetch-depth: 0


name: Check commit message

run: |

commit_msg=$(git log -1 --pretty=%B)

if        !        [[        $commit_msg        =~
^(feat|fix|docs|style|refactor|test|chore)\:        ]];
then

echo "Commit message does not follow conventions"

exit 1

fi
```

```
name: Run tests on each commit

run: |

git rebase origin/main --exec "npm test"


name: Push changes

run: |

git push origin HEAD:${{ github.ref }}
```

Jenkins pipeline for Git-based deployment:

groovy

```
pipeline {

agent any

stages {

stage('Checkout') {

steps {

checkout scm

}

}

stage('Determine Version') {
```

```
steps {

script {

env.APP_VERSION = sh(script: 'git describe --tags --
always', returnStdout: true).trim()

}

}

}

stage('Deploy') {

when {

expression {

return env.GIT_BRANCH == 'origin/main'

}

}

steps {

sh "docker build -t myapp:${env.APP_VERSION} ."

sh "docker push myapp:${env.APP_VERSION}"

sh    "kubectl    set    image    deployment/myapp
myapp=myapp:${env.APP_VERSION}"

}

}

}
```

```
}
```

GitLab CI for monorepo management:

yaml

```yaml
stages:

test

build

deploy


.common_tests:

stage: test

script:

npm test


service_a:

extends: .common_tests

only:

changes:

services/service-a/**/*
```

```
service_b:
extends: .common_tests
only:
changes:
services/service-b/**/*

build_all:
stage: build
script:
./build_script.sh
only:
main

deploy_production:
stage: deploy
script:
./deploy_script.sh
only:
tags
```

Git with Issue Tracking Systems

Deeply integrate Git with issue tracking for enhanced traceability:

Automatically link commits to Jira issues:

bash

```bash
#!/bin/bash

# .git/hooks/prepare-commit-msg


COMMIT_MSG_FILE=$1

COMMIT_SOURCE=$2


# Check if commit is merge or rebase

if [ -z "$COMMIT_SOURCE" ]; then

# Extract Jira issue key from branch name

BRANCH_NAME=$(git rev-parse --abbrev-ref HEAD)

JIRA_KEY=$(echo $BRANCH_NAME | grep -oE '[A-Z]+-[0-9]+')


if [ ! -z "$JIRA_KEY" ]; then

# Prepend Jira issue key to commit message
```

```bash
sed -i.bak -e "1s/^/$JIRA_KEY: /" $COMMIT_MSG_FILE

fi

fi
```

Create GitLab merge requests from Git CLI:

bash

```bash
# Add to .gitconfig

[alias]

mr = !sh -c 'git push -u origin \"$1\" && git lab mr
create origin \"$1\" main -m \"$2\"' -


# Usage

git mr feature/new-feature "Implement new feature"
```

Update GitHub issues with Git notes:

python

```python
# post-commit hook

import subprocess

import requests
```

```python
def get_commit_info():

    commit_hash = subprocess.check_output(['git', 'rev-
    parse', 'HEAD']).decode('utf-8').strip()

    commit_msg = subprocess.check_output(['git', 'log',
    '-1', '--pretty=%B']).decode('ut
```

Chapter 16: Advanced Git Integrations and Ecosystem Tools

Introduction

Git's power extends far beyond its core functionality through a rich ecosystem of integrations and tools. This chapter explores advanced Git integrations and ecosystem tools that enhance productivity, automate workflows, and extend Git's capabilities. We'll delve into how Git interacts with continuous integration and deployment systems, project management tools, code quality platforms, and much more. Whether you're a DevOps engineer, a project manager, or a developer looking to streamline your workflow, this chapter will provide you with in-depth knowledge of Git's extended ecosystem.

Git in Continuous Integration and Continuous Deployment (CI/CD)

Jenkins Integration

Jenkins is a popular open-source automation server that can be tightly integrated with Git for CI/CD workflows.

Configure Jenkins to poll Git repositories:

```groovy
```

```groovy
// Jenkinsfile
pipeline {
agent any
triggers {
pollSCM('H/15 * * * *')
}
stages {
stage('Checkout') {
steps {
git 'https://github.com/username/repo.git'
}
}
// Additional stages...
}
}
```

Use Jenkins Pipeline for Git-based workflows:

groovy

```
// Jenkinsfile
```

```
pipeline {
agent any
stages {
stage('Checkout') {
steps {
checkout scm
}
}
stage('Build') {
steps {
sh 'make'
}
}
stage('Test') {
steps {
sh 'make test'
}
}
stage('Deploy') {
when {
```

```
branch 'main'

}

steps {

sh './deploy.sh'

}

}

}

}
```

Implement Git hooks to trigger Jenkins builds:

bash

```bash
#!/bin/bash

# .git/hooks/post-commit

curl                    http://jenkins-server/job/my-
project/build?token=BUILD_TOKEN
```

GitLab CI/CD

GitLab provides built-in CI/CD capabilities that integrate seamlessly with its Git repositories.

Configure GitLab CI/CD pipelines:

yaml

```yaml
# .gitlab-ci.yml

stages:

build

test

deploy


build_job:

stage: build

script:

echo "Building the project..."

make build


test_job:

stage: test

script:

echo "Running tests..."

make test


deploy_job:
```

```yaml
stage: deploy

script:

echo "Deploying to production..."

make deploy

only:

main
```

Implement GitLab CI/CD for multi-branch workflows:

yaml

```yaml
# .gitlab-ci.yml

stages:

test

build

deploy


test:

stage: test

script:

npm test

only:
```

```yaml
merge_requests

build:
stage: build
script:
npm run build
only:
main
staging

deploy_staging:
stage: deploy
script:
./deploy.sh staging
only:
staging

deploy_production:
stage: deploy
script:
```

```
./deploy.sh production

only:

main

when: manual
```

Use GitLab CI/CD variables for secure configuration:

yaml

```
# .gitlab-ci.yml

deploy:

script:

docker    login    -u    $CI_REGISTRY_USER    -p
$CI_REGISTRY_PASSWORD $CI_REGISTRY

docker push $CI_REGISTRY_IMAGE:$CI_COMMIT_SHA
```

GitHub Actions

GitHub Actions provides powerful CI/CD capabilities directly integrated with GitHub repositories.

Set up a basic GitHub Actions workflow:

yaml

```
# .github/workflows/ci.yml
```

```yaml
name: CI

on: [push, pull_request]

jobs:
build:

runs-on: ubuntu-latest

steps:

uses: actions/checkout@v2

name: Set up Node.js

uses: actions/setup-node@v2

with:

node-version: '14'

run: npm ci

run: npm test

run: npm run build
```

Implement matrix builds for multi-environment testing:

yaml

```yaml
# .github/workflows/matrix.yml

name: Node.js CI

on: [push, pull_request]

jobs:
  build:
    runs-on: ubuntu-latest
    strategy:
      matrix:
        node-version: [12.x, 14.x, 16.x]
    steps:
      uses: actions/checkout@v2
      name: Use Node.js ${{ matrix.node-version }}
      uses: actions/setup-node@v2
      with:
        node-version: ${{ matrix.node-version }}
      run: npm ci
      run: npm test
```

Set up deployment workflows with GitHub Actions:

yaml

```yaml
# .github/workflows/deploy.yml

name: Deploy


on:

push:

branches: [ main ]


jobs:

deploy:

runs-on: ubuntu-latest

steps:

uses: actions/checkout@v2

name: Deploy to Heroku

uses: akhileshns/heroku-deploy@v3.12.12

with:

heroku_api_key: ${{secrets.HEROKU_API_KEY}}

heroku_app_name: "your-app-name"

heroku_email: "your-email@example.com"
```

Git with Project Management Tools

Jira Integration

Integrate Git with Jira for seamless project management and issue tracking.

Link Git commits to Jira issues:

bash

```
git commit -m "PROJ-123: Implement new feature"
```

Set up Jira Smart Commits for updating issues directly from Git:

bash

```
git commit -m "PROJ-123 #comment Implemented the new feature #time 2h 30m"
```

Configure Jira Development Panel to show Git information:

json

```
// Jira application link configuration
{
```

```json
"name": "GitHub",

"type": "github",

"url": "https://github.com/your-org",

"apiUrl": "https://api.github.com",

"clientId": "your-client-id",

"clientSecret": "your-client-secret"

}
```

Trello Integration

Connect Git with Trello for visual project management.

Use Trello Power-Ups to link Git repositories:

javascript

```javascript
// Trello Power-Up configuration

window.TrelloPowerUp.initialize({

'card-buttons': function(t, options) {

return [{

icon: 'https://github.com/favicon.ico',

text: 'GitHub',

callback: function(t) {
```

```
return t.popup({

title: "Link GitHub Issue",

url: './link-issue.html',

height: 184

});

}

}];

}

});
```

Implement Git hooks to update Trello cards:

bash

```bash
#!/bin/bash

# .git/hooks/post-commit

TRELLO_KEY="your-trello-key"

TRELLO_TOKEN="your-trello-token"

CARD_ID="trello-card-id"


COMMIT_MSG=$(git log -1 HEAD --pretty=format:%s)
```

```
curl                     -X                      PUT
"https://api.trello.com/1/cards/$CARD_ID/actions/com
ments" \

-H                "Authorization:              OAuth
oauth_consumer_key=\"$TRELLO_KEY\",
oauth_token=\"$TRELLO_TOKEN\"" \

-d "text=New commit: $COMMIT_MSG"
```

Asana Integration

Integrate Git with Asana for task management and project collaboration.

Link Git commits to Asana tasks:

bash

```
git commit -m "Implement feature X (Asana task:
https://app.asana.com/0/123456789/987654321)"
```

Use Asana's API to update task statuses based on Git activity:

python

```
import asana

import subprocess
```

```
client        =      asana.Client.access_token('your-asana-
access-token')


def update_asana_task(task_id, status):

client.tasks.update(task_id,            {'custom_fields':
{'status': status}})


# Get the last commit message

commit_msg = subprocess.check_output(['git', 'log',
'-1', '--pretty=%B']).decode('utf-8').strip()


# Extract Asana task ID from commit message (assuming
it's in the format "Asana task: 123456789")

task_id    =    commit_msg.split("Asana    task:    ")[-
1].strip()


# Update Asana task status

update_asana_task(task_id, 'completed')
```

Git with Code Quality and Review Tools

SonarQube Integration

Integrate Git with SonarQube for continuous code quality inspection.

Configure SonarQube scanner for Git repositories:

properties

```properties
# sonar-project.properties

sonar.projectKey=my:project

sonar.projectName=My Project

sonar.projectVersion=1.0

sonar.sources=src

sonar.language=java

sonar.java.binaries=target/classes
```

Implement SonarQube analysis in CI/CD pipelines:

yaml

```yaml
# .gitlab-ci.yml

sonarqube-check:

image: maven:3.6.3-jdk-11

variables:

SONAR_USER_HOME: "${CI_PROJECT_DIR}/.sonar"
```

```
cache:

key: "${CI_JOB_NAME}"

paths:

.sonar/cache

script:

mvn    verify    org.sonarsource.scanner.maven:sonar-
maven-plugin:sonar

only:

merge_requests

main

develop
```

Use SonarQube Quality Gates in Git workflows:

groovy

```groovy
// Jenkinsfile

pipeline {

agent any

stages {

stage('SonarQube analysis') {

steps {
```

```
withSonarQubeEnv('SonarQube') {

sh 'mvn sonar:sonar'

}

}

}

stage("Quality Gate") {

steps {

timeout(time: 1, unit: 'HOURS') {

waitForQualityGate abortPipeline: true

}

}

}

}

}
```

CodeClimate Integration

Integrate Git with CodeClimate for automated code review
and quality metrics.

Set up CodeClimate configuration:

yaml

```yaml
# .codeclimate.yml

version: "2"

checks:

similar-code:

enabled: true

config:

threshold: 50

plugins:

eslint:

enabled: true

rubocop:

enabled: true

exclude_patterns:

"test/"

"spec/"

"**/vendor/"
```

Implement CodeClimate in CI/CD pipelines:

yaml

```yaml
# .travis.yml
```

```
env:

global:

CC_TEST_REPORTER_ID=your-code-climate-reporter-id

language: ruby

rvm:

2.7.0

before_script:

curl    -L    https://codeclimate.com/downloads/test-
reporter/test-reporter-latest-linux-amd64   >   ./cc-
test-reporter

chmod +x ./cc-test-reporter

./cc-test-reporter before-build

script:

bundle exec rspec

after_script:

./cc-test-reporter        after-build        --exit-code
$TRAVIS_TEST_RESULT
```

Use CodeClimate badges in Git README files:

```
markdown
```

```
[![Maintainability](https://api.codeclimate.com/v1/b
adges/a99a88d28ad37a79dbf6/maintainability)](https:/
```

```
/codeclimate.com/github/username/repo/maintainabilit
y)

[![Test
Coverage](https://api.codeclimate.com/v1/badges/a99a
88d28ad37a79dbf6/test_coverage)](https://codeclimate
.com/github/username/repo/test_coverage)
```

Gerrit Integration

Integrate Git with Gerrit for advanced code review workflows.

Configure Git to use Gerrit for code review:

bash

```
git config remote.origin.push refs/heads/*:refs/for/*
```

Submit changes for review:

bash

```
git push origin HEAD:refs/for/main
```

Implement Gerrit hooks for automated checks:

bash

```
#!/bin/bash
```

```
# .git/hooks/commit-msg

# Add Gerrit Change-Id to commit message

add_change_id() {

if ! grep -q "Change-Id: " "$1"; then

printf "\n\nChange-Id: I%s" "$(uuidgen)" >> "$1"

fi

}

add_change_id "$1"
```

Git with Container and Orchestration Tools

Docker Integration

Integrate Git with Docker for containerized application development and deployment.

Use Git in Dockerfiles for version control:

Dockerfile

```
FROM node:14

WORKDIR /app

RUN git clone https://github.com/username/repo.git .

RUN git checkout v1.0.0
```

```
RUN npm install

CMD ["npm", "start"]
```

Implement Docker builds in Git CI/CD pipelines:

yaml

```
# .gitlab-ci.yml

build:

stage: build

image: docker:latest

services:

docker:dind

script:

docker build -t myapp:$CI_COMMIT_SHA .

docker push myregistry/myapp:$CI_COMMIT_SHA
```

Use Git commit information in Docker labels:

Dockerfile

```
FROM base-image

LABEL git.commit=${GIT_COMMIT}

LABEL git.branch=${GIT_BRANCH}
```

Build with:

bash

```
docker build --build-arg GIT_COMMIT=$(git rev-parse
HEAD) --build-arg GIT_BRANCH=$(git rev-parse --
abbrev-ref HEAD) -t myapp .
```

Kubernetes Integration

Integrate Git with Kubernetes for GitOps-style deployments.

Use Kustomize with Git for Kubernetes manifest management:

yaml

```
# kustomization.yaml

resources:

deployment.yaml

service.yaml

patchesStrategicMerge:

patch.yaml
```

Implement GitOps with Flux for Kubernetes:

yaml

```
# flux-system/gotk-sync.yaml

apiVersion: source.toolkit.
```

Chapter 17: Git in Specialized Environments and Industries

Introduction

Git's versatility extends far beyond traditional software development. This chapter explores how Git can be adapted and leveraged in specialized environments and industries, each with unique requirements and challenges. We'll delve into practical applications, best practices, and tailored workflows for a variety of fields.

Git in Data Science and Machine Learning

Version Control for Datasets

Implement version control for large datasets:

bash

```
# Using DVC (Data Version Control) with Git

dvc init

dvc add large_dataset.csv

git add large_dataset.csv.dvc
```

```
git commit -m "Add large dataset"

dvc push
```

Managing Machine Learning Models

Version machine learning models:

bash

```
# Using MLflow with Git

mlflow run . -P alpha=0.5 -P l1_ratio=0.1

git add mlruns

git commit -m "Train model with alpha=0.5,
l1_ratio=0.1"
```

Jupyter Notebook Version Control

Effective versioning of Jupyter notebooks:

bash

```
# Using nbdime for notebook-aware diffing and merging

nbdime config-git --enable --global

git add my_notebook.ipynb

git commit -m "Update analysis in notebook"
```

Git in Game Development

Large Asset Management

Handle large game assets:

bash

```
# Using Git LFS for large files

git lfs install

git lfs track "*.psd" "*.fbx" "*.wav"

git add .gitattributes

git commit -m "Set up LFS tracking for game assets"
```

Multi-Platform Development

Manage different platform versions:

bash

```
# Create platform-specific branches

git branch pc-version

git branch mobile-version

git branch console-version
```

```
# Cherry-pick common changes across platforms

git cherry-pick <commit-hash>
```

Modding Support

Set up Git for mod development:

bash

```
# Create a separate branch for mod support

git checkout -b mod-support

git          subtree          add          --prefix=mods
https://github.com/game/mod-framework.git main
```

Git in Hardware Development and Embedded Systems

Version Control for Hardware Description Languages

Manage HDL files with Git:

bash

```
# Set up diff and merge drivers for Verilog files

git          config          diff.verilog.xfuncname
"^(module|task|function|always).*$"
```

```
git config merge.verilog.driver "verilog-merge-driver
%O %A %B %L %P"
```

Firmware Version Management

Track firmware versions:

bash

```
# Tag firmware releases

git tag -a v1.2.3 -m "Firmware release 1.2.3"

git push origin v1.2.3


# Create a branch for each hardware revision

git branch hw-rev-a

git branch hw-rev-b
```

Managing Build Configurations

Handle multiple build configurations:

bash

```
# Use Git worktrees for different configs

git worktree add ../build-debug debug-config

git worktree add ../build-release release-config
```

Git in Regulatory and Compliance Environments

Audit Trails and Compliance Logging

Implement compliant logging:

bash

```
# Use Git notes for audit information

git notes add -m "Reviewed by: John Doe, Approval ID:
12345" HEAD

git push origin refs/notes/*


# Set up a pre-receive hook for compliance checks

#!/bin/bash

# .git/hooks/pre-receive

while read oldrev newrev refname; do

if [[ $refname = "refs/heads/main" ]]; then

if ! git log --format=%B -n 1 $newrev | grep -qE
"Ticket: [A-Z]+-[0-9]+"; then

echo "Error: Commit message must reference a ticket
number"

exit 1
```

```
fi
fi
done
```

Secure Code Signing

Implement code signing for commits:

bash

```bash
# Configure GPG signing for commits
git config --global user.signingkey <your-gpg-key-id>
git config --global commit.gpgsign true


# Sign a commit
git commit -S -m "Signed commit for regulatory
compliance"
```

Access Control and Permissions

Set up fine-grained access control:

bash

```yaml
# Example GitLab configuration for protected branches
protected_branches:
```

343

```
name: "main"

push_access_levels:

access_level: 40 # Maintainers

merge_access_levels:

access_level: 30 # Developers

unprotect_access_levels:

access_level: 50 # Owners
```

Git in Educational Environments

Classroom Assignment Management

Use Git for distributing and collecting assignments:

bash

```
# Create a template repository for assignments

git init assignment-template

touch README.md assignment.py test_assignment.py

git add .

git commit -m "Initial assignment template"


# Student forks and clones the assignment
```

```bash
git clone https://github.com/student/assignment.git

cd assignment

git        remote        add        upstream
https://github.com/teacher/assignment-template.git
```

Collaborative Learning Projects

Set up repositories for group projects:

bash

```bash
# Create a shared repository for a group project

git init group-project

git branch develop

git branch feature-1

git branch feature-2


# Set up branch protection rules

# (Using GitHub API as an example)

curl -X PUT -H "Authorization: token <YOUR-TOKEN>" \

-d
'{"required_status_checks":null,"enforce_admins":tru
e,"required_pull_request_reviews":{"dismissal_restri
ctions":{},"dismiss_stale_reviews":true,"require_cod
e_owner_reviews":true},"restrictions":null}' \
```

```
https://api.github.com/repos/<OWNER>/<REPO>/branches
/main/protection
```

Progress Tracking and Code Review

Implement a code review system for learning:

bash

```bash
# Set up a pre-commit hook for style checking

#!/bin/bash

# .git/hooks/pre-commit

files=$(git  diff  --cached  --name-only  --diff-
filter=ACM | grep ".py$")

if [ -n "$files" ]; then

python -m pylint $files

fi


# Teacher reviews and comments on code

git log -p

git notes add -m "Good use of functions, consider
optimizing the loop on line 23" <commit-hash>
```

Git in Publishing and Content Management

Version Control for Documents and Manuscripts

Manage document versions with Git:

bash

```
# Set up Git for document tracking

git config diff.word.textconv docx2txt

git config diff.word.binary true

git config diff.word.cachetextconv true


# Add a chapter to a book

git add chapter3.docx

git commit -m "Add Chapter 3: Advanced Techniques"


# Create a release branch for editor review

git checkout -b release-v1

git push origin release-v1
```

Collaborative Writing Workflows

Implement a collaborative writing process:

bash

```
# Set up a branching strategy for co-authors

git checkout -b author1-chapter4

git checkout -b author2-chapter5


# Merge completed chapters

git checkout main

git merge author1-chapter4

git merge author2-chapter5


# Use Git LFS for image assets

git lfs track "*.jpg" "*.png"

git add .gitattributes
```

Content Deployment Pipelines

Set up automated publishing workflows:

yaml

```
# Example GitHub Actions workflow for publishing
```

```
name: Publish Content

on:

push:

branches: [main]

jobs:

build-and-deploy:

runs-on: ubuntu-latest

steps:

uses: actions/checkout@v2

name: Build Content

run: |

npm install

npm run build

name: Deploy to CMS

run: ./deploy-to-cms.sh

env:

CMS_API_KEY: ${{ secrets.CMS_API_KEY }}
```

Git in Financial Services

Secure Transaction Logging

Implement secure logging of financial transactions:

bash

```bash
# Use Git for immutable transaction logs

#!/bin/bash

# log-transaction.sh

echo "$(date): $1" >> transactions.log

git add transactions.log

git commit -m "Log transaction: $1"

git tag -a "tx-$(date +%s)" -m "Transaction at $(date)"


# Verify the integrity of the log

git log --show-signature
```

Model Version Control for Quant Trading

Manage quantitative trading models:

bash

```bash
# Version control for trading algorithms

git init quant-models
```

350

```bash
git checkout -b backtest-results

# Log backtest results

echo "Backtest results: Sharpe Ratio 1.5" >> backtest-
log.txt

git add backtest-log.txt

git commit -m "Backtest results for Algorithm v1.2"

# Tag successful models

git tag -a "model-v1.2" -m "Validated model with
Sharpe Ratio 1.5"
```

Compliance and Audit Workflows

Set up Git workflows for financial compliance:

bash

```bash
# Pre-commit hook for sensitive data check

#!/bin/bash

# .git/hooks/pre-commit

if git diff --cached | grep -E
"API_KEY|SECRET|PASSWORD"

then
```

```
echo "ERROR: Attempt to commit sensitive data"

exit 1

fi


# Post-commit hook for compliance logging

#!/bin/bash

# .git/hooks/post-commit

echo "$(date): $(git log -1 --format="%H") - $(git
config user.name)" >> compliance-log.txt
```

Conclusion

This chapter has demonstrated the versatility of Git across
various specialized environments and industries. From data
science to financial services, Git's core principles of version
control, collaboration, and traceability can be adapted to
meet diverse needs. As you apply these techniques in your
specific field, remember that Git's flexibility allows for
continuous innovation in how it's used. Stay curious,
experiment with new workflows, and always seek to
optimize your version control processes for your unique
requirements.

Chapter 18: Advanced Git Techniques and Integrations

Introduction

As we reach the pinnacle of our exploration into Git, it's time to delve into the most advanced techniques and integrations that this powerful version control system offers. This chapter is designed for those who have mastered the fundamentals and are ready to push the boundaries of what Git can do. We'll explore complex scenarios, advanced features, and integrations that can significantly enhance your development workflow. By the end of this chapter, you'll have a deep understanding of Git's internal workings and be equipped to tackle even the most challenging version control situations.

Git Internals and Plumbing Commands

While most Git users interact with the system through its porcelain commands (high-level commands designed for everyday use), understanding Git's internals and plumbing commands can provide you with powerful tools for advanced operations and troubleshooting. Git's object model, consisting of blobs, trees, commits, and tags, forms the foundation of its functionality. By exploring these internals, we can gain insights into how Git manages and tracks changes, enabling us to perform low-level operations when needed.

Understanding Git Objects

Git's object database is at the core of its functionality. Every file, directory structure, and commit in Git is represented as an object, each with a unique SHA-1 hash. There are four types of objects in Git: blobs (file contents), trees (directory structures), commits (snapshots with metadata), and tags (references to specific commits). Understanding how these objects relate to each other is crucial for advanced Git operations. For example, a commit object points to a tree object, which in turn points to blob objects representing file contents. This structure allows Git to efficiently store and retrieve different versions of your project.

To explore Git objects, you can use the `git cat-file` command. For instance, to view the contents of a commit object:

bash

```
git cat-file -p <commit-hash>
```

This command will display the commit message, author information, and the tree object that the commit points to. By following the chain of objects, you can traverse the entire history of your repository at a low level.

The Git Index

The Git index, also known as the staging area, is a crucial intermediate step between your working directory and the Git repository. Understanding how the index works can help you manage complex staging scenarios. The index is essentially a binary file that stores a list of file paths and their corresponding object hashes. When you stage changes using `git add`, you're updating the index with new object hashes. The `git ls-files` command can be used to inspect the contents of the index:

bash

```
git ls-files --stage
```

This command will show you the mode, object hash, stage number, and file path for each entry in the index. Advanced users can manipulate the index directly using plumbing commands like `git update-index` for fine-grained control over what gets committed.

Refs and the Reflog

Git's references (refs) are pointers to commits, and understanding how they work is essential for advanced branching and history manipulation. The `.git/refs` directory contains files representing branches, tags, and remote references, each containing the hash of the commit they point to. The HEAD reference is special, as it points to the current branch or commit. The reflog, a log of reference updates, is a powerful tool for recovering from mistakes or understanding how your repository's state has changed over time. To view the reflog:

bash

```
git reflog
```

This command shows a list of times when the HEAD reference was updated, along with the corresponding commit messages. You can use this information to recover lost commits or branches, even after seemingly destructive operations like a hard reset.

Advanced Rebase Techniques

Rebasing is a powerful Git feature that allows you to modify your commit history. While basic rebasing is straightforward, advanced techniques can help you solve complex problems and maintain a clean, linear history. Interactive rebasing, in particular, offers a high degree of control over your commit history.

Interactive Rebase

Interactive rebasing allows you to modify a series of commits in various ways. You can reorder, edit, squash, or even delete commits during the rebase process. To start an interactive rebase:

bash

```
git rebase -i <base-commit>
```

This command opens an editor with a list of commits and instructions. You can change the command for each commit to modify how it's handled during the rebase. For example, you can use `squash` to combine commits, `edit` to pause the rebase and make changes, or `reword` to change commit messages. This powerful feature allows you to clean up your commit history before merging or pushing, ensuring that your project history is clear and meaningful.

Rebasing with Autosquash

The autosquash feature can significantly streamline your workflow when you need to make small fixes to previous commits. When you make a commit with a message starting with "fixup!" or "squash!" followed by the subject line of a previous commit, Git can automatically reorder and combine these commits during an interactive rebase. To use this feature:

```
bash
```

```
git commit --fixup <commit-hash>

git rebase -i --autosquash <base-commit>
```

This technique is particularly useful when you discover small bugs or typos in previous commits and want to fix them without cluttering your history with additional fix commits.

Rebase Onto

The `git rebase --onto` command allows you to move a series of commits from one base to another. This advanced technique is useful in scenarios where you want to change the parent of a series of commits. For example:

bash

```
git rebase --onto <new-base> <old-base> <branch>
```

This command takes all commits between `<old-base>` and `<branch>` and replays them on top of `<new-base>`. This can be particularly useful when you've branched off the wrong branch and need to move your work to a different base.

Advanced Merging Strategies

While basic merging is a common operation in Git, there are advanced merging strategies and techniques that can help you handle complex integration scenarios more effectively. Understanding these advanced merging concepts can significantly improve your ability to manage complex codebases and collaborate with large teams.

Octopus Merge

An octopus merge is a merge that brings together more than two branches simultaneously. While not commonly used, octopus merges can be useful in certain scenarios, such as when you need to integrate changes from multiple feature branches at once. To perform an octopus merge:

bash

```
git merge branch1 branch2 branch3
```

This command will create a new merge commit with multiple parent commits. Octopus merges are best suited for situations where the branches being merged have no conflicting changes. If conflicts occur, Git will abort the octopus merge, and you'll need to resolve the conflicts manually using multiple two-way merges.

Recursive Merge Strategy

The recursive merge strategy is Git's default strategy for merging branches. It's called "recursive" because it can handle multiple merge bases in cases where the branches have diverged and then been merged back together. This strategy is highly effective at resolving complex merge scenarios. You can explicitly specify this strategy using:

bash

```
git merge -s recursive branch-name
```

The recursive strategy also supports several options that can be useful in specific scenarios. For example, the `ours` and `theirs` options allow you to automatically favor one side's version in case of conflicts:

bash

```
git merge -X ours branch-name
```

This command will resolve all conflicts in favor of the current branch's version.

Subtree Merging

Subtree merging is an advanced technique that allows you to merge one repository into a subdirectory of another repository. This can be useful for managing complex project structures or incorporating external projects into your own. To perform a subtree merge:

bash

```
git        remote        add        -f        subproject
https://github.com/example/subproject.git

git  merge  -s  subtree  --squash  --allow-unrelated-
histories subproject/main
```

This sequence of commands adds the subproject as a remote, then merges it into a subdirectory of your main project. The --squash option combines all of the subproject's commits into a single commit in your main project, which can help keep your history clean.

Git Hooks and Automation

Git hooks are scripts that Git executes before or after events such as commit, push, and receive. They provide a powerful mechanism for automating tasks and enforcing policies in your Git workflow. By leveraging hooks, you can significantly enhance your development process, ensure code quality, and maintain consistency across your team.

Client-Side Hooks

Client-side hooks run on the developer's local machine and can be used to enforce coding standards, run tests, or perform other checks before commits or pushes. Some commonly used client-side hooks include:

pre-commit: Runs before a commit is created, useful for linting and style checks.

prepare-commit-msg: Runs before the commit message editor is started, can be used to generate or modify commit messages.

post-commit: Runs after a commit is created, useful for notifications or triggering local builds.

Here's an example of a pre-commit hook that runs tests before allowing a commit:

```
bash
```

```
#!/bin/sh

# .git/hooks/pre-commit


npm test


if [ $? -ne 0 ]; then

echo "Tests failed. Commit aborted."

exit 1

fi
```

This script runs your project's tests and aborts the commit if any tests fail, ensuring that only code that passes tests is committed.

Server-Side Hooks

Server-side hooks run on the Git server and can be used to enforce project-wide policies or trigger actions when repositories are updated. Common server-side hooks include:

pre-receive: Runs when the server receives a push, before any refs are updated.

update: Similar to pre-receive, but runs once for each ref being updated.

362

post-receive: Runs after a successful push, useful for triggering deployments or notifications.

Here's an example of a post-receive hook that triggers a deployment:

bash

```sh
#!/bin/sh

# .git/hooks/post-receive

while read oldrev newrev refname
do
branch=$(git rev-parse --symbolic --abbrev-ref $refname)
if [ "$branch" = "main" ]; then
echo "Deploying main branch..."
/usr/bin/deploy-script.sh
fi
done
```

This script checks if the pushed branch is "main" and triggers a deployment script if it is.

Git Attributes for Automation

Git attributes allow you to specify attributes for paths in your repository, which can be used to configure how Git handles certain files or directories. This can be particularly useful for automating tasks like line ending conversion, diff generation for binary files, or applying filters. To use Git attributes, create a `.gitattributes` file in your repository:

```
*.txt text

*.jpg binary

*.data filter=crypto
```

This example sets text files to have normalized line endings, marks jpg files as binary (preventing Git from trying to merge them), and applies a "crypto" filter to .data files. You can then set up custom filters or diff drivers to handle these files specially.

Git for Large Repositories and Monorepos

As projects grow in size and complexity, managing them with Git can become challenging. Large repositories and monorepos (repositories containing multiple projects) require special techniques to maintain performance and usability. Git provides several features and best practices to help manage these large-scale repositories effectively.

Git Large File Storage (LFS)

Git LFS is an extension that replaces large files in your repository with text pointers, storing the actual file contents on a remote server. This can significantly reduce the size of your Git repository and improve performance. To use Git LFS:

bash

```bash
git lfs install

git lfs track "*.psd"

git add .gitattributes

git commit -m "Configure Git LFS for PSD files"
```

This sequence of commands sets up Git LFS and configures it to track PSD files. When you add and commit PSD files, Git LFS will handle them specially, storing them separately from the main Git object database.

Partial Clones and Shallow Clones

For very large repositories, cloning the entire history may be impractical. Git offers partial clones and shallow clones to address this issue. A partial clone allows you to clone a repository without downloading all the blob objects:

bash

```bash
git clone --filter=blob:none https://github.com/example/large-repo.git
```

This command clones the repository without downloading any file contents, fetching them on-demand as needed. A shallow clone, on the other hand, limits the number of commits fetched:

bash

```
git clone --depth 1 https://github.com/example/large-repo.git
```

This clones only the most recent commit, significantly reducing the amount of data transferred and the local storage required.

Monorepo Management Techniques

Managing a monorepo requires careful consideration of repository structure, build systems, and Git usage patterns. Some techniques for effective monorepo management include:

Using Git submodules or subtrees for independent components

Implementing sparse checkouts to work with subsets of the repository

Utilizing custom build systems that understand the monorepo structure

Employing advanced branching strategies to manage multiple projects

Implementing rigorous code review and testing processes to maintain quality across the entire repository

By combining these techniques with Git's advanced features, you can effectively manage even the largest and most complex repositories.

Conclusion

This chapter has explored some of the most advanced Git techniques and integrations available. From diving into Git's internals and using plumbing commands to implementing complex automation with hooks and attributes, we've covered a wide range of topics that can significantly enhance your Git workflow. As you apply these advanced techniques in your projects, remember that with great power comes great responsibility. Always consider the impact of your actions, especially when modifying history or implementing server-side hooks that affect your entire team. With these advanced skills at your disposal, you're now equipped to tackle even the most complex version control challenges and optimize your development workflow to its fullest potential.

www.ingramcontent.com/pod-product-compliance
Lightning Source LLC
LaVergne TN
LVHW051428050326
832903LV00030BD/2962

*9 7 9 8 3 4 3 0 0 5 3 2 5 *